D0115940

A Gospel of Hope

Also by Walter Brueggemann
from Westminster John Knox Press

A Gospel of Hope

WALTER BRUEGGEMANN

Compiled by Richard Floyd

WESTMINSTER
JOHN KNOX PRESS
LOUISVILLE · KENTUCKY

First edition
Published by Westminster John Knox Press
Louisville, Kentucky

18 19 20 21 22 23 24 25 26 27—10 9 8 7 6 5 4 3 2 1

Book design by Sharon Adams
Cover design by designpointinc.com
Cover illustration: © Tina Gutierrez

Library of Congress Cataloging-in-Publication Data

Names: Brueggemann, Walter, author.
Title: A gospel of hope / Walter Brueggemann.
Description: Louisville, KY : Westminster John Knox Press, 2017.
Identifiers: LCCN 2017047280 (print) | LCCN 2017049861 (ebook) | ISBN 9781611648492 (ebk.) | ISBN 9780664262280 (hbk. : alk. paper)
Subjects: LCSH: Christian life. | Faith. | Hope—Religious aspects—Christianity.
Classification: LCC BV4501.3 (ebook) | LCC BV4501.3 .B7765 2017 (print) | DDC 230—dc23
LC record available at https://lccn.loc.gov/2017047280

PRINTED IN THE UNITED STATES OF AMERICA

Most Westminster John Knox Press books are available at special quantity discounts when purchased in bulk by corporations, organizations, and special-interest groups. For more information, please e-mail SpecialSales@wjkbooks.com.

Contents

Preface

There is a certain audaciousness in gathering up one's words from former times and presenting them again. As I reread my words from former times, it strikes me that there is some audaciousness in their first utterance. In them I have said things well beyond my understanding. But then it occurs to me that my words (and my ministry) belong to a long chain of audaciousness that in turn is rooted in the audaciousness of the biblical witnesses themselves. (I have in mind a parallel to André Brink's *Rumors of Rain: A Novel of Corruption and Redemption*.) It is amazing to ponder what it was like when Moses (or "J") or Amos or "Job" or Paul or Mark had their say the first time. In their very utterances they generated worlds that did not exist prior to their utterances. Such utterances have indeed called "into existence the things that do not exist" (Rom. 4:17). It is indeed, as the hymn "Morning Has Broken" proclaims, all "fresh from the word." And that is why we utter and keep uttering and reutter and listen for more.

Without such utterance and reutterance, our lives regress to what is safe, conventional, and routine. These bold agents of utterance intend, in every utterance, to awaken us from our "dogmatic slumbers" and from the temptation to have our faith reduced to a privatized narcotic.

When we push these utterances back far enough, we reach back to the generative utterance of God that every time is a world-generating, world-changing act. Imagine what it was like for this holy God to say:

> Let there be light!
> Let my people go!
> Let justice roll down like mighty waters!
> This is my beloved Son!
> Love one another!
> Fear not, I have called you by name!

Every such utterance merits an exclamation point!!

To be sure, they are only utterances, even the ones that come from God. In hearing them, however, over time we discover in them a transformative reality that always runs beyond our capacity to explain them or control the futures they create. For that reason, I am glad to be a wee part of that chain of audacity in which we people of faith stand, a chain that gives us an assurance that passes all human understanding and a mandate that leaves us, at our best, as restless odd misfits in the world. In retrospect my timid audacity is a bid that the church and its pastors should marvel at and respond to this long chain of words that summons us to glad, obedient risk. In our present moment such a summons is urgent, both because our society has clearly lost its way in a frenzy of alienation and anxiety and because old familiar modes of faith are not adequate, as the hymn "God of Grace and God of Glory" attests, for "the living of these days."

As I reread my words I came to be concentrated on two familiar lyrical texts in the New Testament. First, Paul's great benediction in Ephesians:

> Now to him who by the power at work within us is able to accomplish abundantly far more than all we can ask or imagine, to him be glory in the church and in Christ Jesus to all generations, forever and ever. Amen. (Eph. 3:20–21)

The apostle knows the power of God to be effectively active in the life of the world, an effective action in abundance. The human counterpoint to God's effective abundance is to "ask or imagine." This is not a discouragement or limit on our asking from God or our imagining about God. It is rather, I suggest, an invitation that we should be asking from God and imagining about God extravagantly. Our text affirms we must not curb our asking or our imagining but recognize the inadequacy of our asking and imagining. God still surprises us with more and better. It is not fashionable in progressive circles to imagine that God can do "abundantly." Consequently we ask only anemically of God because we do not trust much in God's agency. It is not fashionable in conservative circles to ask or imagine God's goodness beyond a rigid calculus of obedience.

But this fact simply makes clear how progressive and conservative Christians stand together before the mystery of God, who outruns all of our timid calculus, whether the rationalism of progressives or the moralism of conservatives.

The other text that has come to my mind is the famous inventory of Hebrews 11:

> Now faith is the assurance of things hoped for, the
> conviction of things not seen. (Heb. 11:1)

"Faith" in the rhetoric of this text is not a package of
certitudes or a trusted mantra. It is rather reliance on
and trust in a future-giving, future-hoping God who
constantly makes a way out of no way. Thus faith, in this
verse, promptly morphs into hope for the future that
will be unlike the present. What follows in the chapter
is a roll call of hopers who have refused the status quo
because they trusted that God has "something better"
for those who are courageously able to move on. Hope,
in Hebrews 11, is not a head trip or a heart trip; it is a
body trip of putting one's body at risk for the sake of new
possibility. Ta-Nehisi Coates (*Between the World and Me*)
has reckoned whites to be something like "body snatch-
ers" who want to possess and occupy black bodies. For
most of us our bodies (thus our lives) are held in thrall
by safe domestication. But here in Hebrews 11 are the
names of those who have risked their bodies for the sake
of the future. This roll call is pertinent for our dangerous
time, and one wonders whose names are yet to be added
to that roster.

It is my hope that these reuttered words of mine might
serve as a contribution to the audacity of our talk and
our walk. This dangerous time calls folk of faith to grow
in our awareness and courage to subvert "by thought,
word, and deed" (*Book of Common Prayer*) current ideolo-
gies that want to curb and administer our asking and our
imagining.

I am grateful to Richard Floyd for his ready energy and
discerning discipline to select from my many words these
for reutterance. He has entered into my mind enough
to know what I most want to say, and into my rhetoric

enough to know how I am most likely to say it. He has aided me in making my contribution to the chain of audacity in which we have the glad chance to participate.

Walter Brueggemann
Columbia Theological Seminary
July 5, 2017

Chapter One

Abundance and Generosity

I invite you to keep this question before you: What are you after? And what would it mean to eat the real food of covenantal faithfulness, to receive and accept it, to live it and give it, to be transformed and weaned away from the stuff that only makes you more hungry?

❧❧❧❧❧❧❧❧

When we do not trust in guaranteed abundance, we must supply the deficiencies out of our own limited resources. We scramble to move from our sense of scarcity to an abundance that we imagine that we ourselves can supply, all the while frantically anxious that we won't quite make it: It is necessary to erode the holy time of Sabbath for the sake of productivity, given our sense of scarcity grounded in distrust.

❧❧❧❧❧❧❧❧

We baptized people are the ones who have signed on for the Jesus story of abundance. We are the ones who have decided that this story is true story, and the four great

1

verbs—he took, he blessed, he broke, he gave—constitute the true story of our lives. As a result we recognize that scarcity is a lie, a story repeated endlessly, in order to justify injustice in the community.

We have in our baptism declared the old story of scarcity to be false. And we have become the people and the place in the city where abundance is practiced. We notice that we have more than we need. We notice that we do not need to keep so much for ourselves. We notice that as we share, more is given. We notice that every time we commit to the truth of abundance, new energy, new joy, and new well-being surge among us.

❧❦❧❦❧❦❧❦❧

Commodity thinking says that you share with your neighbor stuff that you can afford. Covenantal thinking says that you share first with your neighbor, and then you and your neighbor live on what you've got together.

❧❦❧❦❧❦❧❦❧

Jesus has come that we may have an abundant life. His feeding narratives attest that the generosity of God is assured wherever Jesus rules in the earth, and we count on that generosity. And that means that our common practices of greed, of the pursuit of consumer goods, of the frantic effort to acquire more, are both inappropriate and unnecessary. Our society hungers always for more: more body surgery, more cosmetics, more cars, more beer, more sex, more certitude, more security, more money, more power, more oil . . . whatever.

This hunger for more is a true sign that we do not trust the goodness of God to supply all of our needs; we do not trust that the generous rule of Jesus who has ascended to power is in effect. But we, we are Jesus people, and therefore we are pledged and empowered to act differently, differently in the neighborhood, differently in the economy, and as citizens of the last superpower, differently in the world.

※※※※※※※※

Our exhaustion, I propose, is rooted in anxiety that mistrusts the abundance that God has ordained into creation and, as a result, we—like the creator on the sixth day—have our spirits completely depleted. But we, unlike the creator, take no seventh day for refreshment, because, unlike the creator, we are too anxious to rest. And he says, "Come to me, all you that are weary." True creatureliness, like birds and lilies, trusts the abundance of the Father. But we imagine we know better in our wisdom and in our intelligence. We spend ourselves in the futility of trying to take the place of the life-guaranteeing God.

※※※※※※※※

When you are full, do not forget. Being full causes amnesia. Being comfortable causes indifference. Being secure makes us unresponsive.

※※※※※※※※

There are enough flocks and herds and fish, because this is the creator God, the one who keeps on giving gifts. Prophets are those who complain about their work, threaten to quit, and face God when God is pissed off. But the call is to vouch for enough in a world of fearful anxiety. The people around Moses were weary with what they had. They complained. They complained for a lack of fish and cucumbers and melons and leeks and garlic and onions. In their scarcity they became restless and contentious and romanticized the past, because scarcity does that. It produces greed and anxiety and often violence. It results in selfish budgets and privatization. It produces violence and meanness and parsimony and anti-neighborliness and road rage and class warfare against the poor.

And right in the middle of that, God revs up prophets who ask the right questions and know the faithful answer: enough!

Enough grace to include all!

Enough neighborliness to restore safety and dignity!

Enough resources to share with widows and orphans and immigrants!

Enough of pruning hooks and plowshares that we need not take up the arms of sword and spear.

Enough that we need not scandalize the poor with our selfishness.

Enough that we need not live with grudge and resentment and fear, as though we were under threat.

Enough bread broken and wine poured out to exhibit gifts and give thanks.

⚜⚜⚜⚜⚜⚜⚜⚜

We exist because of God's inscrutable generosity in our creation, a generosity so rich that we need not be greedy or self-sufficient, because gifts are always being given. That story has its hope and culmination in the promise that God will make all things right, and that our destiny is to be in peaceable communion with God and with our neighbors, in this age and in the age to come. And between our beginning in generosity and our culmination in communion, our lives are lived in glad, obedient response to God's purpose in our lives.

❖❖❖❖❖❖❖❖

Now I want you to think what happens when we forget, what happens when we give up the story and we think we are too sophisticated, when we practice amnesia. I will tell you what happens. We give up on the wonder of abundance. We neglect God's miracle of generosity. And we start imagining that there is scarcity of food, of love, of life.

And driven by scarcity, we scramble to get ours and more and more, climbing over and through and upon our neighbors to get ours. It is the case that our Western economy is rooted in a claim of scarcity and so we scramble. The poor scramble with robbery and violence and threat. The powerful scramble with investments and tax advantages and credit and exploitation. And together the rich and the poor create a jungle of anxiety, brutality, and violence. That is what forgetting will surely produce. And what is true in our culture is also true more closely in the family that operates on zero-sum love.

But we remember. And so we know that a life and an economy driven by scarcity is a fraud. And we remember to break ourselves away from the fraud of scarcity. We remember the gospel that there is enough, food is given, God is generous. The task of remembering is to break away from the grip of scarcity that holds us in bondage.

❖❖❖❖❖❖❖❖

It is odd to talk about self-discipline in a therapeutic, self-indulgent culture of limitless consumerism that is on an endless binge of self-satisfaction. The news is that there is an alternative to all of that; it is rooted in the gospel. Christian people who are serious about Jesus have always been invited to a more excellent way of deliberately saying "yes" and deliberately saying "no" about time and about money, about speech, about neighbor, about sexuality, about charity, about hospitality, about all those things that make us human. [Imagine] a church that is so clear on its holy calling, so sure of its identity in the world that it is not indulgent and flabby and slovenly about its identity or its mandate.

❀❀❀❀❀❀❀❀❀

Imagine a group of people who no longer meet to sing and dance and remember fidelity. In that world, memory is lost and amnesia is the order of the day, forgetfulness that assumes that we are the ones and only ones, none before us, none to come after us, only us, free to use up all of creation . . . and its oil!—in our own extravagant way. Moses, of course, knows all about this; he knows that affluence breeds amnesia and the loss of a grounding memory:

> When you have eaten your fill and have built fine houses and live in them, and when your herds and flocks have multiplied, and your silver and gold is multiplied, and all that you have is multiplied, then do not exalt yourself, forgetting the LORD your God, who brought you out of the land of Egypt, out of the house of slavery. . . . Do not say to yourself, "My power and the might of my own hand have gotten me this wealth." But remember the LORD your God, for it is he who gives you power to get wealth, so that he may confirm his covenant that he swore to your ancestors, as he is doing today. (Deut. 8:12–14, 17–18)

❀❀❀❀❀❀❀❀❀

The enduring act of love is generosity. The world teaches us to be selfish and stingy and to look out for ourselves. But gospel love is grounded in the conviction that all we have is a gift from God who has been generous with us and we are invited to practice generosity alongside the God of the gospel. We imagine, in our relative wealth, that we are not so rich. But in fact, when love is at work we need very little, much less than we imagined. And then we are free, as free as Jesus was free, to pass it along.

❧❧❧❧❧❧❧❧❧

Jesus has an antidote to anxiety. The antidote is abundance, the outpouring of generosity of the creator God, the gift that keeps on giving. That is the antidote to anxiety! It is the acknowledgment of the creator God. The world is not left on its own. The world is not turned loose with its own limited resources. The market is not an autonomous agent in the world. There is the Father God who outruns all the power of anxiety and overwhelms with abundance.

❧❧❧❧❧❧❧❧❧

I assume you are something like me. You find yourself pulled in two directions, or you find yourself haunted by two different versions of your life. One story that competes for our loyalty is the money story as it is told and lived in the modern world. That is the story of self-sufficiency and hard work and competence and merit and being safe on our own terms. The sign of that story is more—more goods, more influence, more alcohol, more stock options, more power, more published articles, more running shoes, more chemical dependence, more trips to Europe, more capital gains—whatever. It is a tale that insists that no matter how much one gathers together, it is not yet enough for happiness and safety. But more will make us happy and secure.

I assume you are like me—you know about the power and attractiveness of that story, and at least some of the time are drawn to it.

But we know about and take seriously a quite different account of our lives; we are haunted by this other account, drawn to it, and on a good day, intend to put our lives down in that other version of reality. This is the story of the gospel. It is an account of God's generosity that we are able to see in the mystery of God's creation, that we know crucially in God's love in Jesus of Nazareth, and that we trust because we have experienced it in intimate, concrete ways in our own lives.

※※※※※※※※

You, dear brothers and sisters, are the ones entrusted with the mystery of abundance that you yourself first may believe. The drama of abundance, whereby the creation bears its fruit in extravagance, is precisely enacted in the Eucharist. Holy Communion is not about sin and salvation. It is about the wonder that God the creator has moved directly against all our anxiety to overwhelm us with reliable abundance.

※※※※※※※※

In the face of "road rage" that is rooted in anxiety and that takes for itself unexamined high moral ground, there is this old, deep gift of being irenic according to the gospel. Such a practice as an evangelical alternative is not just because we are "good guys," or because "anything goes" and we can be lukewarm and indifferent about great issues. It is rather, as Paul knew so well, that we are rooted in God's gracious generosity; our life does not finally depend upon our being in control or our being right. The primal business of our life is to yield in trust to the God who loves us more than we love ourselves.

❖❖❖❖❖❖❖❖

Our memory is saturated with promises still being kept. But in our amnesia, the promises seem neither interesting nor credible. And when we cease to trust promises and no longer hope, we end in despair, for despair is the counter to hope. And despairing people act greedily, because we believe God has no new gifts to give.

Consider: Our memory is saturated with free bread, all gift rooted in God's generosity. But amnesia crowds against free bread and we cannot remember bread given. We do not believe that "loaves abound." And so we conclude in our failed memory, that there is a scarcity of bread. We scramble to keep all our bread we have. We intrude on our neighbors and take their bread too. Until they have no bread and we have no neighbors, because we cannot remember miracles named gratitude.

❖❖❖❖❖❖❖❖

Where there is no sacrament that dramatizes the world as a mystery of abundance, life becomes sheer commodity and human transactions are reduced to market transactions. Matters we have traditionally understood as social goods—medical care and education, for example—now become only tools of leverage in the service of greed.

❖❖❖❖❖❖❖❖

What is our life about? It is not about accumulation and control and self-sufficiency. In that way lies death. In the midst of that failed ambition, the voice of Jesus is a voice of another way of work and rest that takes into account our true character. In our several exhaustions, we are invited to rethink, to work differently without so many expectations, and to rest in joy and well-being, unafraid.

❧❧❧❧❧❧❧❧

There is a generosity of the spirit in the gospel, a generosity not overpowered by our fears, a generosity that is not compromising on the basics, but open to folks who come in many shapes and sizes. It is finally this gospel-based generosity that will still our fears, curb our anger, quench our brutality, and make us new. In the end, all of us crave enough forgiveness and the gift of freedom to get through the day and sleep in the night. And now it is promised: At-homeness for all, all of us, here alive, today. It is promised to those who continue to do the hard work of old passions that permit new decisions.

❧❧❧❧❧❧❧❧

The burden of what Jesus says is this: give it away. Give it away gladly. Make friends by your generosity. The door to a gospel future is by generosity, outrageous, intentional giving away in the present to create a viable future. That seems to me such an urgent word, because we are so deeply caught in cycles of greed and affluence and self-indulgence and acquisitiveness of a fearful kind that will yield no human future.

❧❧❧❧❧❧❧❧

There is the frightened notion that it all belongs to us and there are neither gifts we need to receive nor miracles to which we need to respond. For such people, there is no generosity, only grudging fear. Soon comes time for church people to pledge time, energy, and money for the work of the church. That is when we decide if we can join the new song. The world resists such a song. But those of us who come to the table are called into these wonders; we are among those who sing the new song and bring an offering deeply out of our poverty. God's generosity invites our generosity.

✤✤✤✤✤✤✤✤✤

The world is under new governance. This is authentic regime change. Receive the kingdom of abundance and do not engage with the gods of scarcity. Serve the God of neighborly righteousness and quit worrying about all the threats and competitors. Give your life over to God's will for the neighborhood, as an act of generosity, and all the rest comes, all the rest about which you have been anxious—your life, your food, your drink, your clothing, your house.

Chapter Two

Alternative Worlds

The world comes at us in destructive, pathological ways. From out of the chaos, however, comes this other voice rooted in memory. Comes the text shaping our future not in hostility but in compassion, not in abandonment but in solidarity, not in isolation but in covenant, not in estrangement but in well-being.

❧❧❧❧❧❧❧

There is nothing ordinary about the key claims of biblical faith. Indeed, there is almost nothing about biblical faith that can be understood according to our usual analytical, scientific, objective, or common-sense control of life. The Bible is, rather, organized around the explosive moments when the holiness of God touches down in our midst and changes everything. Such touch-down moments are not sweet and romantic. They are not pious and religious. Rather, they are moments of threat and risk, when our worlds are shattered and everything is changed.

❧❧❧❧❧❧❧

As we sing our life out toward God, who is our shepherd and our king, we sing the center of our life away from ourselves. As we sing life toward God and away from ourselves, we sing away from the fear and anxiety that causes us to act in selfish and inhumane ways. For which of you, by turning to self, can add a cubit to your life? As we sing life toward God, we announce that the selfish, greedy ways of our culture are false. We announce to the world that the mad arms race toward security is a lie, because it will never make us safe. We declare that consumerism is a lie, because we can never eat enough and have enough to make us safe. We receive well-being only from this other one to whom we turn in praise.

❧❧❧❧❧❧❧❧❧❧

There is a countertruth that surfaces in Christian worship. It is a small counterpoint without great voice or muscle. It has been a minority perspective for a very long time. The ones who practice the counterpoint know very well that ours is not and will not be a dominant voice. It is a sub-version of reality, one that sounds beneath the loud sounds of the dominant version, one that flies low beneath the radar surveillance of the dominant version.

In every liturgical utterance, act, and gesture, this sub-version of reality intends to subvert dominant versions, to expose them as inadequate if not false, and to empower the community to reengage reality according to this sub-version.

This delicate tension between dominant version and sub-version, I believe, is the true character of worship. The claims made in the sub-version, claims such as "Christ is risen," are a deeply felt, eagerly offered truth. And yet in its very utterance the community at worship knows that the facts on the ground, the data at hand, contradict this and give evidence that the odor of death is still very much in play. It will not do for the church to become cynical and give in to the dominant vision. But it also will not do for the church to become excessively romantic about its sub-version and so to imagine its dominance. Rather, I believe that the worshiping community must live knowingly and elusively in this tension, not cynical, not romantic, but wise and innocent (Matt. 10:16), always engaged in negotiation between sub-claim and the world the way we find it.

❧❧❧❧❧❧❧❧

Dominant culture imagines a centered, secure, well-ordered world that permits absolutes and certitudes, and a deep sense of coherence about the world. This is fed and reinforced in the United States by the imperial practice of hegemony in military and economic terms that imagines security is established by having our way everywhere in the world. No displacement here!

Dominant culture imagines a normative security of legitimacy and conformity that enforces norms about life, finance, the military, and sexuality and imposes a high degree of conformity on all members of the community. It is impatient with those who do not submit and conform and who practice and advocate deviation from consensus norms. No "other" here!

Dominant culture is largely committed to acquisitiveness and to the uncriticized centrality of the market. Such acquisitiveness pertains not only to the economy, but to all social relationships including those of sexuality, a point indicated in characteristic soap operas, survival shows, and "comedies" that are characteristically marked by aggressive attitudes and mean-spirited interaction which is said to be "entertaining." No covenant here!

Dominant culture is committed to 24/7 about everything, about work, about play and self-indulgence, about instant availability by cell phone or whatever. There is no space left for the human spirit, and attentiveness to the underneath mystery of human life is totally eroded. No Sabbath here!

Dominant culture is a culture of assertive initiative taking without any openness for mutuality or mood or practice of receptivity. No yielding prayer here!

⚜⚜⚜⚜⚜⚜⚜

We are in process of deciding, to whom does the present belong? On most days, we imagine, the present belongs to the empire. When we think that, we succumb in resignation, because then we conclude that everything is settled and nothing can be changed. On some days, however, we hear this voice which crowds in on the empire. That odd voice, the voice of the gospel, asserts, "I am doing a new thing. Do you notice?" When we notice, we are strangely free. We sing, we dance, we care—with abandonment— because we are no longer intimidated. We get our strength back. We get our priorities right. We declare God's praise and reclaim the present for the God to whom it belongs We are liberated to live in the present where God's newness is at work, undaunted, undiminished, unintimidated, free, powerful, joyous. It is enough to trust the poem and to find the present made new for God's purpose.

⚜⚜⚜⚜⚜⚜⚜

Ours is a time like the flood, like the exile, when the certitudes abandon us, the old reliabilities have become unsure, and "things fall apart." The falling part is happening for conservatives, and it is happening for liberals. It is happening all around us, and to all of us.

In such a context of enormous fearfulness, our propensity is to enormous destructiveness. Grow more strident, more fearful, more anxious, more greedy for our own way, more despairing, and consequently, more brutal. That propensity to destructiveness is all around us. On many days we succumb to its power; we succumb to the need to look only after ourselves and our kind, only selfishly, only ideologically, only "realistically."

The alternative is an act of imagination seeded by memory, uttered by a poet that draws the health-giving memory into the present, so that the present is radically reconstituted. Such an act of imagination is not shaved down to fit our realism, or to conform to our interest, or to accommodate our conventional reality. We do not need poetry or artistry or imagination, if we only want to wallow in our status quo. The poet stakes a claim against such present reality. This act of imagination subverts our status quo and invites us to an alternative.

⚜⚜⚜⚜⚜⚜⚜

When the truth is told, a new world remains possible.

⚜⚜⚜⚜⚜⚜⚜

The subversion of faith has nothing to do with being liberal or conservative. It has to do rather with this question: whether the dominant force of technological, electronic, military consumerism is to have the final say in the world, whether the practices of greed, alienation, despair, amnesia, and brutality are to be the shape of the world in which only the privileged have a chance to live well, and that, by utilization of the deprivileged as a means toward ends. Or whether the covenantal dreams of Moses, the deep hopes of Jeremiah, and the suffering, transformative love of Jesus will draw us to an alternative faith that treasures our common, God-given humanness.

❧❧❧❧❧❧❧❧❧❧

We beguile ourselves in our ostensible well-being that we are immune from and unrelated to the terrible inhumanity that reaches the news. The New Testament knows that we hold membership in the world of injustice, implicated by our birth, by our baptism, our citizenship. The New Testament church knows that Jesus' people suffer, not because such suffering is noble or pious or sadistic, but because the claim of truth by Jesus puts us into deep conflict with the way power is arranged in the world.

I do not imagine that what is needed is heroic action. I do not imagine that what is required is young people to rush off to causes. Rather we are at the hard work, to see how faith in this crucified-risen One dares a clear vision of reality, how the truth of Jesus challenges or agrees with other truth, how our easier truth in the world is so readily tied to privilege and advantage and power.

❧❧❧❧❧❧❧❧❧❧

The church, by its words and by its odd acts of generosity and emancipation, opens the world to new possibility that makes all the old possibilities impotent. . . . The powers of death did their best—or their worst—on Friday; those powers could not prevail. They are shown to be helpless before God's power for life. And so the church continues to mock death and to celebrate God's gift of life that will not be defeated.

❧❧❧❧❧❧❧❧❧❧

As Paul speaks of the God of hope who gives new futures out of love, he knew about a world of despair

that trafficked in brutality. And so do we. The world
of despair believes that there are no new gifts, no fresh
generosity, no possibility of newness or forgiveness, and
so life becomes a zero-sum game to see who can stay
the longest on top of the heap, all the while knowing
that there will be no good outcome to the futile rat race.
Well, here is the news. Out beyond that despair that
sanctions road rage and violence against the poor and
war and ruthless exploitation that leaves one exhausted
if not half dead, there is an alternative world bodied in
Jesus. It is a world of new gifts and fresh starts grounded
in divine forgiveness and sustained by generosity. That
world is on offer in this one who is about to be born
among us.

❧❧❧❧❧❧❧❧❧

In the community of faith, to "imagine" does not mean
to "make up." It means, rather, to receive, entertain,
and host images of reality that are outside the accepted
given. If, however, we say "receive" images, then we may
ask, "receive from whom?" Or "receive for whom?" The
answer we give is that what the Psalmists and liturgists
imagine and shape and offer is given by God's spirit,
for it is the spirit who bears witness. It is the spirit that
has given Israel freedom to recognize and acknowledge
Yahweh as savior from slavery. It is the spirit that gives
us eyes to see and selves to notice the recurring and con-
stant fidelity of God. It is the spirit that cries out with
us, that lets us cry out and receive God's rescue. It is the
spirit that moves in the faith of the community and in
the artistry of the poet to give voice to the odd truth of
our common life.

❧❧❧❧❧❧❧❧❧

You disciples, you have seen. You have known; you have been in his presence. You have been healed and fed by him. You have tasted his bread and drunk his wine. You know!

You know about life rooted in the spirit of God and not in the spirit of the age of violence.

You know about the poor and have not had your head turned by wealth and power.

You know about the impulse of creation toward health, a creaturely health signed in bread and wine. You know. And because you know you keep on singing. You can keep singing. You can keep hoping. And because you sing and hope, you can act in freedom, unburdened, unco-erced, unafraid and without cynicism. The song goes on. It is a subversive, revolutionary song. And we, given access to this odd king, get to sign on to sing and to live it—unafraid!

⚜⚜⚜⚜⚜⚜⚜⚜

There is a new world available that is here very soon. It is being birthed in the wonder of Jesus of Nazareth. It is a world marked by the stable smell of shepherds and the perfumes of the wise men. It is a world marked by a Friday of suffering and death and by a Sunday of surprise and new life. It is a world that exposes all of the contra-dictions of our present life. It is a world that invites us to move out from here to there in joy, in obedience, in discipline, to begin again.

⚜⚜⚜⚜⚜⚜⚜⚜

We are required to look carefully. We are called to train our eyes to see differently, to see what the world does not notice. The newness of the gospel may take many forms:

a child, a cup of water, an old lady who shares, a harlot
who risks, a new law, a new budget item, an odd risk for
an institution. Newness is any surprising move toward
justice, mercy, and compassion.

❧❧❧❧❧❧❧❧❧

God is everlasting and has made the world. That's polem-
ical. It means the Babylonian gods are not to be trusted
because they can't really do anything. Don't accept the
claims of those other gods. It is simply true that no economic system can finally give us life. No security system
based on fear can ever make us safe. No social arrangement that displeases God can ever let us be human. We
have believed the world too much. We have listened
to the Babylonians. We have yearned too much for the
American dream. And people who get caught in Babylonian dreams or American dreams wind up without
energy for faith and mission. But as we focus on the God
who is free and restless and at work, we break the spell of
the empire, and we are free again.

❧❧❧❧❧❧❧❧❧

What Jews and Christians have in common—alone and
with no one else—is that we believe that there is one
who is coming to make the world right. We believe
that God has not quit on the world, and has not given
up on God's own will for the world and God's promise
to make the world whole and safe and peaceable. We
believe that because of God's steadfastness, the world
will not remain a killing field of violence and brutality
and hate and fear.

❧❧❧❧❧❧❧❧❧

The world does not need the church to talk about what is already possible. The work of the church is to battle the world's definition of what is believable and unbelievable.

⚜⚜⚜⚜⚜⚜⚜⚜⚜

Christians are blessed when they maintain an awareness and a practice of the present that remembers that this is not how God wills it. But Jesus not only reads the present in a different way. Jesus also invites his disciples to a different take on the future. Jesus invites his disciples to be with him in the promises of God, knowing that God will do new, healing things in the world, new Easter deeds that the world does not imagine, because God has not yet quit on bringing the world to newness.

⚜⚜⚜⚜⚜⚜⚜⚜⚜

Those of us who have grown up in the church have had a good fill of the notion that the world is bad, it is tempting, it is filled with demons and sinners, and the good man is the one who can endure it until we reach our other home. Now perhaps few of us believe that, and yet there is always a haunting reminder that we are not meant for this place. And now we are called by the gospel to put away such negative and paralyzing views of the world, which do not stop us from living, but prevent us from the joy we may have.

⚜⚜⚜⚜⚜⚜⚜⚜⚜

The key religious question among us is whether there is ground for an alternative, an alternative rooted not in self-preoccupation or in deadening stability, but rooted in a more awesome reality that lives underneath empires, that comes among us as odd as a poem, as inscrutable as power, as dangerous as new life, as fragile as waiting. The poet names the name and imagines new life, like eagles flying, running, walking.

❖❖❖❖❖❖❖❖❖

God has drawn a line against the destructive darkness; and we are invited to answer the light. It is against the darkness that God has said no stealing, no killing, no adultery. It is against barbarism that God has said no slander, no false witness, no gossip. This community of faith has learned that when we disengage from our deathly, self-seeking ways, God's gift of light and life comes. But the light requires self-surrender. The life requires the loss of our selfish, controlling ways. . . . God intends to reorder our common life on new terms.

❖❖❖❖❖❖❖❖❖

We have learned—and keep needing to relearn—that the cross is not simply a one-time deal in the life of Jesus or of God. Rather the cross is the clue about how to live an alternative life in the world, an alternative life that is marked by risky innocence that has the power to heal, to create caring neighborhoods in the face of rapacious markets, to evoke new possibilities in the face of despair, to enact new forms of liberation in the face of endless locks of oppression. The clue of course is that none of this happens, unless there is a risk of self, so that the enhancement of the neighborhood requires the expenditure of self.

❖❖❖❖❖❖❖❖❖

The simple claim of our faith is that Jesus of Nazareth destabilizes the human world, makes something new happen that is human, and requires us to get on with life in a new way. So the real issue is not, how do miracles happen? The real issue is, what shall we do with Jesus? Shall we trust him like the man and obey him like the spirit and be raised? Or shall we continue in our recalcitrant disbelief that leaves the world closed and close to death?

❧❧❧❧❧❧❧❧❧

Jesus summoned and constituted an alternative community of which we are heirs. Imagine that a small community set down in the midst of the empire and all of its aggressive militarism is a small community that refuses to participate in the anxiety of the world, because it imitates birds and lilies in the sure confidence that the Father in heaven knows our needs and supplies them.

❧❧❧❧❧❧❧❧❧

Our faith holds deep, central, and nonnegotiable that God will form a new human community. We do not know how. In our situation, as in every frightening situation, it is easier to think those promises of newness are simply old traditional promises but have now been outrun in our technological capacity for destruction. It is tempting to imagine that the loss may be true, but the promises are not operative. It is easier to conclude there will be no joyous after, no voice of bride and bridegroom. But there it is, perched on the lips of Jesus, "You will laugh," because God's will works a human community, we know not how. He countered the doubt by saying tersely, "If you laugh now you will end crying." If you celebrate what is, you won't receive what will be. If you are deeply committed to the old world ending, you won't be present or available for the new world God will put into the void of creation.

Chapter Three

Anxiety and Freedom

Jesus exactly contrasts "anxiety" and "the father God" who knows all our needs. It is an elemental lack of trust in the creator God—elemental distrust that is the common human predicament but that is enhanced for us as children of the Enlightenment—that leads to Sabbath-negating anxiety. Jesus invites his disciples into anxiety-negating Sabbath, grounded in abundance, about which birds and flowers know, that refuses the scarcity imagined in our autonomy.

⚜⚜⚜⚜⚜⚜⚜⚜

As you know, we live in a fearful society that is devoured by anxiety. And we imagine in our anxiety that there are extreme "security" measures that will make us safe. But if this is God's world and if the rule of love is at work, then our mandate is not to draw into a cocoon of safety; rather, it is to be out and alive in the world in concrete acts and policies whereby the fearful anxiety among us is dispatched and adversaries can be turned to allies and to friends.

⚜⚜⚜⚜⚜⚜⚜⚜

Being unafraid is an odd vocation; but it is the vocation of all those who have been baptized. We are different when baptized. The Acts account of the early church says that the Spirit of God came upon the ones baptized, even as the Spirit came upon Jesus in baptism. A lot of silliness is taught about the Spirit coming in baptism. But what the Spirit does is visit our lives—our persons, our bodies, our imagination, our money—with the freedom of God, so that we are unafraid in the world, able to live differently, not needing to control, not needing to dominate, not needing to accumulate, not driven by anxiety.

⚜⚜⚜⚜⚜⚜

Stewardship is a resolve to move beyond the tale of anxiety. We imagine that more will end our anxiety. But it will not. It will only make us more anxious. We end our anxiety by drinking the waters that will quench, even in danger, and are satisfied. Stewardship is not about cunning budgets. It is about being our true selves, rooted in generosity, destined for communion, privileged with neighbor in the present tense.

⚜⚜⚜⚜⚜⚜

The church is called to be an odd presence that is the only chance for humanness beyond the deathly flow of anxiety that is all around us. The ones who are un-anxious can spend growing portions of their life in vulnerable companionship, and so the church watches the command to love flow out beyond itself into the community. That command to love one another shows up in acts of compassion and mercy, in a passion for justice and equity, in freedom for eating and singing and dancing that defies the empire.

⚜⚜⚜⚜⚜⚜

I assume we are all alike in the way we are variously compromised and fatigued. Does this ring true for you?

1. That we have enough stress from getting through the day that we do not have excessive energy left for singing and dancing and leaping high. We are stressed by the economy, by the rat race, by shortages in the church, and by the demands from insistent kids that we sometimes get wrong before the day runs out.

2. That we are complicated and compromised. It would be nice and noble to "will one thing." But we do not, for the most part, will one thing. We are double-minded about our conflicted lives of having enough for ourselves and giving it away, of being forgiving and holding to standards, of cutting corners and being straightforward. This is the human predicament and it is, give or take, our predicament as well.

3. That we are gripped by fear at least some of the time, fear of failure, fear of running out, fear of letting people down, fear of not measuring up. Or the big fears about nuclear power and the environmental mess up and the loss of our pensions.

4. That we are largely burdened with the present tense, so that present circumstance seems all encompassing and present obligations feel defining for us.

❧❧❧❧❧❧❧❧

Ours is a time of upheaval and threat and challenge, when people are devoured with anxiety. The world seems strange, and nothing stays the way it used to be. We are dwarfed by huge concentrations of power and wealth and are helpless before them. We are minimized by technological capacities and electronic advances that seem to rob us of initiative in our own lives. Consequently, when we are devoured by anxiety and dwarfed by bigness and minimized by technology, people do strange and mean and destructive things to each other. It is as though God has put us into a craziness, and this God has called the church to be an un-anxious presence in the midst of this society.

❊❊❊❊❊❊❊❊

Jesus interrupts the fearmongers and says to his disciples, "Do not be anxious. Do not fear." Jesus invites his listeners into another zone, not of magic or of superstition or of supernaturalism, but into the evangelical reality that the world will hold. It will not fall apart. As a result, we can get our minds off ourselves and live our lives in glad obedience that is rooted in gratitude.

❊❊❊❊❊❊❊❊

Be in a mode of "fear and trembling" before the holy presence of God and fear nothing else. Tremble before none other and be on your way—you who live outside the world's zone of anxiety. Be on your way, rejoicing.

❊❊❊❊❊❊❊❊

Jesus took the form of a servant and became obedient unto death. The disciples were astonished. How could he do that? Why would he do that? And the answer is that his life is freed, from the beginning and from the end, by the truth of the God who is full of grace. A well-framed life permits vulnerability; a life framed by self and for self ends in fear and such needful self-preoccupation that we can never take off the outer robe, can never kneel, can never come empty-handed to the folks with dirty feet. He acted out for them (and for us) the freedom of a life framed in the gospel.

❊❊❊❊❊❊❊❊

Do not sacrifice your life for the old gods of coercion and anxiety. Rather notice the God of impossibility. Among us this God gives life to the dead and calls into existence things that do not exist. Even among us! We are invited to dwell in God's freedom!

⚜⚜⚜⚜⚜⚜⚜⚜⚜

The good news is that Yahweh, the God of the exodus, is in charge. All creatures can be their true selves, without fear or failure. Trees can be happy trees, bearing fruit and giving shade. Fields can be productive fields. Oceans can be fruitful, restored oceans, the earth can be its fruitful self. And we share the joy, because if this God is God, we can be our true selves, free of hate and rage and guilt and alienation. We can be the true best selves that God has intended and hoped we would be. No wonder the whole world dances. The good news of the gospel is that because this God is really God, we can be our true selves, healed, whole, joyous, free, trusting, and obedient. The gospel is very good news. We receive it with joy. We can leave off the old patterns of twisting ourselves in false ways. Such distortions are no longer necessary, because the old, fake loyalties have been nullified. We are free and long for the way to the well-being God wants to give.

⚜⚜⚜⚜⚜⚜⚜⚜⚜

The reason there is such craziness, such a binge of fear and hate, such a propensity to brutality and violence and terror and counterterror . . . the reason is that people are anxious down to the very bottom of their lives. Anxious people, when their anxiety is strong and deep enough, do crazy destructive things to each other and to themselves, which in any other context would be shameful and unacceptable. Such deep anxiety causes us to divide the world into "us and them," into good guys and bad guys, and then imagine that we are good and right and pure and righteous—all because of anxiety. But it is not so in the faithful church. . . . And the reason it is not so? The reason is: We Christians are not like our society. The reason is: We are un-anxious in an anxious society. . . . Un-anxious because of the faithful presence of God in Jesus Christ in whom we trust. . . . Take deep notice of the ways in which we are different, because of the truth of the gospel, the truth of God's Easter victory over all that threatens our lives and our world. That is what the word "evangelical" means . . . to trust ourselves to the truth of the gospel!

❀❀❀❀❀❀❀❀❀

The good news of Jesus counters the deep fear of death in our society. In a world where the God of the living is not known or trusted, we use much energy fending off death, trying to stay young, trying to stay beautiful, trying to stay fit, trying to stay healthy, and if not young and beautiful, and fit, and healthy, then at least rich, in order to be safe. But all this frantic attempt to enhance life is, in the end, futile. For death, as life, is in God's hands. And we are safe.

❀❀❀❀❀❀❀❀❀

Despair, you see, is not an affliction of the down and out-ers. Some who are down and out and who have reason, do indeed despair. But the great pathology of despair afflicts the affluent who imagine that we have everything we are going to get. When we no longer have gifts to receive, we may cease to enter the gates with thanksgiving. We may no longer make a joyful noise, because we want to keep quiet and conform and be docile so that we do not disrupt. In our culture we are nearly being done in by our technology, which locks everything in place. Wouldn't it be a great surprise to discover that the technology in which we so much trust turns out to be a tool of despair, because it reduces possibility to the system.

❖❖❖❖❖❖❖❖❖

We are given an assurance by Jesus for the long run: God is the God of the living. Beyond that, however, we are given freedom for the short term, enabled by this news of God to live our life differently, to use our time, energy, and resources out beyond ourselves, precisely because the well-being of ourselves is already assured, and we need use no energy on that. It occurs to me that Jesus' assurance, "God is God of the living," is thus also a summons, an invitation, an imperative, "be sure you are among the living," be alive to the life that God permits you.

❖❖❖❖❖❖❖❖❖

What is it that makes people like us weary? It is not working too hard that makes us weary. It is rather, I submit, living a life that is against the grain of our true creatureliness, being placed in a false position so that our day-to-day operation requires us to contradict what we know best about ourselves and what we love most about our life as children of God. Exhaustion comes from the demand that we be, in some measure, other than we truly are; such an alienation requires too much energy to navigate.

❖❖❖❖❖❖❖❖❖

If you cringe at the boisterous, cocky new sound of religion in politics, if you worry about the divisiveness of

"red" and "blue," and if you are vexed that too many people claim to be speaking directly for Christ: you might
think that our Christian faith is all about getting the
moral issues right and leveraging others to think and act
the right way, as do we. But if you think that, you are very
wrong, because such contemporary loud posturing is not
so much about faith as it is about anxiety and maintaining
control in the world. Our faith, I propose, is not about
pinning down moral certitudes. It is, rather, about openness to wonder and awe in glad praise.

✵✵✵✵✵✵✵✵

We do not want to choose decisively between the dominant script of therapeutic technological consumer militarism and the counterscript of the elusive, irascible God.
Most of us vacillate or mumble in our ambivalence. This
ambivalence takes a conservative form of attentiveness to
personal and familial stuff with the public sphere left to
the ideology of the market. This ambivalence takes a liberal form with a subjective consciousness so that there is
an urbane, ironic filter between what we say and what we
mean. The ambivalence touches every church member,
liberal and conservative, and engrosses every minister of
whatever ilk.

It is the anxiety about our double-mindedness that
becomes the grist of ministry that makes us fearful and
strident and adversarial. It is our anxiety that causes us to
enlist as red or blue ministers in red or blue churches. It
is our anxiety that precludes the ease of Sabbath, the dal-
liance of birds, the leisure time of lilies.

There is, of course, an antidote, even if it is given in
patriarchal form: "For it is the Gentiles who strive for all
these things; and indeed your heavenly Father knows that
you need all these things" (Matt. 6:32).

And we are left, post-anxiety, with only God's realm and God's righteousness.

❈❈❈❈❈❈

Because the future belongs to God and because he will be gracious to us in that future, we don't need always to be calculating for our well-being, our safety, our prosperity, our security, our reputation. All these concerns can be trusted to God. And we are freed to care about other matters, namely the things which belong to God's future. Our society is beset with terrible preoccupations about the future and our survival. But Christian faith is not a promise that we shall survive or be happy or get a payoff. It is rather the affirmation that we are freed from those questions, that we can worry about the future and what it can become, because all the maintenance problems have been taken care of.

❈❈❈❈❈❈

It is the command of Jesus that we not worry, as the world worries, in ways that make us crazy or mean or angry or hateful or quarrelsome. It is a command spoken by Jesus who himself is un-anxious and unflappable. Indeed, it is difficult to imagine Jesus being anxious. He is unafraid before the Roman governor at his trial, unflappable before the high priests on his dread-filled Thursday inquisition, unworried when the storm rages, completely at peace even in the ferocious storm on the Sea of Galilee. He is unafraid, un-anxious, not worried. And he invites his disciples to stay close to him, and to share his un-anxious presence.

❈❈❈❈❈❈

The truth is that frightened people will never turn the world, because they use too much energy on protection of self. It is the vocation of the baptized, the known and named and unafraid, to make the world whole.

❧❧❧❧❧❧❧❧❧

Every community now is worried, because the old ways do not work anymore. And in their anxiety, communities are tempted to all kinds of controlling regulations and figure out ways to be exclusive in order to keep out the "others" and let life be undisturbed and uncomplicated, as though that would make us safe. All around the local community is fear, a fear that keeps being fed by the fearful, about immigration, about the economy, about oil, about terrorists, all kinds of manipulatable fears that turn us into a worried, even paranoid society. But the church speaks another word in such a context. It is a word of preaching and living, of witnessing and acting, that we are unafraid and we invite the world to be unafraid with us.

❧❧❧❧❧❧❧❧❧

Jesus knew that he had come from God, to whom he belonged. He knew where his roots were. He had come from Nazareth, or from Bethlehem. He had come from strong old Jewish stock. But that is not really where he came from. What he knew for sure is that he came out of God's love that had cherished him since the foundation of the world before his being named, before his being birthed, before he was conceived, he was inscribed into the very fabric of the creation that the creator loves. He had been created, he had been loved into existence and could fall back in confidence into that reliable love where he was known and safe and valued. He is such a contrast to those of us who are so consumed in our anxiety and so eaten up by fear that we do not know where we have come from or to whom we belong.

Jesus knew he was going to God. He knew his future. He did not speculate about resurrection or immortality or life after death or the second coming or such close religious parsing of God's promises. He knew that God was God, full of grace and truth, and that God would abide and govern after all the threats had been emptied of their poison. He knew even before the catechism was written that his only source of comfort and strength in this world and in the world to come is that he belonged to his faithful creator God. He knew that his destiny was well-being in the communion of saints, where all is forgiven and there is joy and peaceableness. The folk who are anxious and restless and on edge do not know that they are going to God and will be safe there. They imagine they are only going to their own possessions and security, because they imagine that we are all on our own in the world.

❧❧❧❧❧❧❧❧❧

God did not say, "seek me in chaos." Embrace the chaos, face it full and acknowledge it. But do not be excessively fascinated by the loss, failure, and brutality. Do not linger there too long as though that is God's place of disclosure. Instead watch for God to move powerfully out beyond the chaos to form a new world, a new community, new persons, new possibility.

❧❧❧❧❧❧❧❧❧

We are the weary ones whom Jesus invites in gentleness, "Come to me, all you that are weary and are carrying heavy burdens, and I will give you rest" (Matt. 11:28), because we are overly busy and overly anxious about the maintenance of our world. We are overly busy and overly anxious because we believe that one more call, one more meeting, one more performance review, one more check to make sure the lights are out and the dishes washed and the mail answered, one more anything will make this a better place and enhance our sense of self.

But of course it is never enough, for our anxious sense of responsibility will never touch the truth of creation. For the truth of creation, without any regard for us or our need to make it right, is that God has ordained the world in its abundance; it will perform its life-giving exuberance without us, as long as we do not get in the way.

❧❧❧❧❧❧❧❧❧❧

Where the God of the gospel comes, lives are trans-formed and we have the freedom and courage to live a self-surrendering life, and we do so in gladness. Jesus always comes and says, "Fear not," and invites us to fall back in trust, so safe, so valorized that we need not think about ourselves. He comes and says, "My peace I give you." Fear is indeed cast out.

❧❧❧❧❧❧❧❧❧❧

There is a power beyond fear. There is a gift of self-giving love. There is a baptism. There is new news. There is a commandment for the new life. Fear keeps welling up among us with authority. But the baptized resist it. There is, we now know, a more excellent way to live, to hope all things, to endure all things. This way never ends; it is a gift that keeps on giving.

Chapter Four

God's Fidelity and Ours

Talk about death and resurrection is not funeral talk, or speculation about "life after death." It is rather Easter talk. It is waiting for and receiving the power of new life, new energy, new courage, and freedom, permission to be the real you, permission you have not been willing to receive, the courage to be the faithful church, no longer bogged down in our usual pettiness, the capacity to be a genuinely humane community, overriding our greed, our fear of brutality, "coming home with shouts of joy" (Ps. 126:6).

❧❧❧❧❧❧❧❧

God has located the seeds of new life just where we would never think to look for them. In the Christian tradition, of course, we dare say that the blessing of God is located in the life of Jesus, whose life is bracketed in powerlessness between Herod at the beginning and Pilate at the end. But the whole world turns to him like the final centurion and says, "Bless me."

The drama of blessing, so poignant in Jesus, is not confined to the body of Jesus. It is also at work, according to

God's odd calculus, wherever the failed, emptied forms of power must come in petition to the hidden, unnoticed carriers of life. It is such a scandal, but then our faith is built on the scandalous affirmation that the power of God is given in hiddenness, so that more blatant forms of power must come and finally say "bless me."

❧❧❧❧❧❧❧❧❧

There is something tough and starchy and uncompromising about God, who finally will enact heavy-duty sovereignty in the historical-political process when the mocking has gone on long enough. When great power violates the flow of God's history, it will come to deep trouble and destructiveness.

❧❧❧❧❧❧❧❧❧

Faith is not a warm, cuddling self-indulgence that causes us to cheat on the hard questions. Faith rather offers a body of conviction that helps us see clearly. Truth is not an embrace of a bunch of facts or theories in the name of some pretended objectivity. Truth rather is the genuine shape of reality before it has been skewed by our bias or seized by our vested interest. The church has long claimed that its faith is an invitation to see the world clear and whole and honest.

❧❧❧❧❧❧❧❧❧

When [the disciples] ask for more faith, he answers, it takes only faith the size of a mustard seed. It takes just a little, a little faith, a little trust in God, a little confidence in God's goodness, a little readiness to stay in gratitude, and you can make a massive difference in the world by breaking the cycles of destructiveness. Jesus talked about moving a tree, moving something we think is immovable, a big tree of hate, a mountain of rage, an ocean of bad behavior, because the power of generosity and reconciliation is such a staggering moral force in the world, such a fit of unexpected loveliness, and it breaks the grip of deathliness.

⚜⚜⚜⚜⚜⚜⚜

Healing is the strange act of the power of life being present in the midst of the power of death, or more simply and directly, healing consists in human life making contact with human life, and finding together the gift of new possibility strangely given.

⚜⚜⚜⚜⚜⚜⚜

Praise is an abrasive announcement that this is God's world. It leaves us open to God's gift of spirit. It leaves us open to God's summons to obedience. It leaves us open to God's promised kingdom. When doxology is not sung, we shrivel and grow brutish and fearful. When we praise, we have a chance at our vocation in God's image.

⚜⚜⚜⚜⚜⚜⚜

The character of God given us in Jesus is so overwhelmingly powerful for the care of life, not only in this age, but in the age to come, that we may be sure about the long term, for the long term is safely in God's good hands.

⚜⚜⚜⚜⚜⚜⚜

God is not a blind principle of fate. God is not a remote threat or an indifferent power. God's whole life is marked by God's inclination to be with us and for us, to do us well.

⚜⚜⚜⚜⚜⚜⚜

God's capacity for fidelity fills the whole of creation, the heavens, the clouds, the mountains, so that all of life is redefined apart from scientific, geological, measurable, controllable objects into the categories of relationship. What counts for the shape of reality is trust, and the capacity to let God's good mystery permeate and saturate all of life. The world oozes in all its parts with God's faithfulness.

❖❖❖❖❖❖❖❖❖

The one to whom we pray is indeed steadfast, compassionate, faithful, merciful. This God is so loyal that we are invited to end our atheism, to come home from our distorted selves and from our destroyed, dysfunctional community. This God is one of glorious light, enough to enlighten and enliven our way.

❖❖❖❖❖❖❖❖❖

We, in our society and in our churches, are sore tempted to monologue. Such a temptation imagines absolute certainty and sovereignty, and uncritically imagines that any one of us can speak with the voice and authority of the monologic God. Such certitude is an act of idolatry.

In the public arena, the military-economic hegemony of the United States exercises a monologic practice of power that by force imposes its will on others and silences voices to the contrary. The same propensity is evident in government that is now largely co-opted and controlled by wealthy interests that amount to nothing less than an oligarchy wherein voices of need can scarcely be heard. It is not, in my judgment, very different in the churches, wherein judgments are made and positions taken that make sounds of absolute certainty without any sense either that God's own life in the world is dialogical or that there is inevitable slippage between God's will and our perception of that will.

Yet unless we know that God is dialogical, we will never understand that truth takes dialogical form among members of church and society in a way that precludes ready settlement. Such a theological awareness requires among us a huge unlearning of conventional monologic theology in the church. The manifestation of a dialogical God becomes the premise for dialogic human community that precludes both absolute authority and absolute submissiveness.

❧❧❧❧❧❧❧❧

The deep reality of divine abandonment did not lead to silence and resignation. Rather, it led to vigorous protest, accusation, and petition that eventuated in divine attentiveness. And if we wonder why abandonment led to speech, it is because everything in this dialogic community leads to speech. Israel knows, and after Israel, Sigmund Freud and Martin Luther King and many others, that utterance produces newness. Utterance enlivens social possibility, but it enlivens social possibility because we—all of us—are in the image of the dialogic God. Praise, the alternative voice of this community, is not easy speech; it arises only after the hard trouble is told, truth that is hard on all powerful ears, including the ears of the powerful God.

❧❧❧❧❧❧❧❧

We know because of God's amazing gifts to us that rules are interesting but not primary.

❧❧❧❧❧❧❧❧

It is our testimony that one cannot live a faithful, productive, joyous life unless one has grace and truth—fidelity and reliability—at one's core. Of course that is what we have meant by the Reformation accent on unmerited grace. It is what Augustine meant by his lovely phrasing, "Our hearts are restless until they find their rest in thee." We are watching—in personal and in public spheres—the fruition and the effects of self-serving. Indeed we have known from the ground up that such efforts cannot work and are no viable substitute for grace that is inherent in the processes of creation and history. Even in our culture that is now so profoundly secular and disoriented, it continues to be the case that grace and truth are the irreducible foundations for a livable, sustainable human life.

✢✢✢✢✢✢✢

There are those among us who are touched by the graciousness of God, and find in that touch a warrant for caring inclusiveness. And there are also those among us who take up the wild severity of God, and read from it an agenda of demanding, impatient moral distinctiveness. It can hardly be otherwise. If we insist that heaven does come to earth, what we get is not only the wondrous solidarity of forgiveness, but also the starchiness of God's holiness. The program of severity is difficult for us to bear, because it does spin off into intolerant human claims, with just enough warrant to make it as dangerous and compelling as God's own claim.

The theological task, given this unresolved state of God, is not simply judicious believing and detached adjudication. It is rather advocacy born of Moses's hutzpah, to storm into the very core of God's life and insist on plan A, and to storm the very courts of life in the world and insist that God's truth as healing is a profound claim in the face of God's well-discerned severity.

✢✢✢✢✢✢✢

In the interpretative imagination of Israel, everything that happens is read as a sign and signal of Yahweh's abiding fidelity (*hesed*); the world and its historical processes are known to be saturated with divine constancy and stability.

⚜⚜⚜⚜⚜⚜⚜⚜⚜

The God who dispatches us into discipleship and exile and missional risk, the God who has in mind that we be present at the breaking points of injustice, at the open wounds of alienation and despair, the God who puts us there, is the mother God who comforts. Being comforted by the presence of God is an alternative to our quest for being comfortable. The gospel is always against our being comfortable, in order to be comforted in our dis-ease. I invite you to think about this terrible distinction between being comfortable and being comforted, between our capacity to cope and our willingness to be held and embraced, to be nursed and cared for and suckled by this God who now speaks and holds us midst our dark night of ache, holding our bodies that tremble with the tears of fatigue and despair.

This mothering God . . . who says "comfort" only in the midst of exile, who drops the shrill tone only when we are lean and needful, this oddly available God is known to us in text and tradition, in creed and song and sacrament, but finally is known in hidden communion when we take time in our discomfort to be held in the secret place of our hurt.

⚜⚜⚜⚜⚜⚜⚜⚜⚜

Goodness, assurance, well-being are not established by us as a gift to God, something we offer, but it comes to us, a gift to us, God's way of letting us, as we are, be all right. Jesus himself alone is God's gift of well-being that we receive in faith, opening ourselves to the real oddity of Jesus that is grace.

❧❧❧❧❧❧❧❧❧

In the conversation of life and faith, this other voice of steadfastness has been speaking from all eternity, long before we spoke, long before we hurt. God's steadfastness does not intrude late, only at a desperate last moment, if at all. God's fidelity has been there first, uttered over us before we knew how to petition or complain or pray or hope. God's first decisive speech is always reverberating—and that powerful assertion changes the way we speak, even about loneliness and violence.

❧❧❧❧❧❧❧❧❧

Amnesia eventually creates a lostness when life is lived outside the arena of fidelity to God who is our true home. When the stories are not known, life and money and power and sexuality will be organized without reference to the holiness of God, and that way lies destruction.

❧❧❧❧❧❧❧❧❧

The deep truth of our faith and our memory is that we are called away from our own life to God's life and then sent back to our life differently. Our life is not our own. We are not free to do what we want, and we are not abandoned to do what we want. We are held safely in the hands of a God who knows better how we shall live toward wholeness, well-being, and joy.

❧❧❧❧❧❧❧❧❧

God's speech changes our speech. God's word transforms our talk. God's reality changes our very life. The hurt, failure, restlessness, and fear are still there, but now they are contained in God's mercy which is wider than the sea. What we celebrate in our regular worship is that our speech is serious life-and-death speech, bound in a certain conversation. The talk here is always of fidelity and faithfulness and forgiveness, of being healed and held and made whole, of beginning again.

⚜⚜⚜⚜⚜⚜⚜⚜

To be our best true selves in a best true world means to live a life of deep fidelity, faithful to self, faithful to neighbor, faithful to God. People like us can have our life changed. We can live differently because this different God governs.

⚜⚜⚜⚜⚜⚜⚜⚜

This is an invitation to tilt our life toward the powerful reality of God. It is our life's work to so tilt our life. We are not our own. We did not make ourselves. We cannot finally care for ourselves. Our lives belong to God and exist for God's wondrous purposes. That is the good news. Our task of faith is to find ways to lose our life in joy and obedience, in praise and prayer, and to find life given us beyond our best hope.

⚜⚜⚜⚜⚜⚜⚜⚜

Take the yoke of Jesus. Take his yoke upon you. "Yoke" means rule or discipline or production schedule. Most of us have fallen into yokes that are demanding, that rub our necks and our lives sore and keep us exhausted. Take instead the yoke of Jesus, for that burden is easy and the yoke is light. It is the yoke of discipleship. It has its demands. This invitation of Jesus is not cheap or free. But its demands are of another sort, not competence, not productivity, not conformity, but the freedom to address your neighbor's life in caring ways.

When we take the yoke of Jesus and trade it for our thousand other yokes of slavery, there is rest from futile work. It is not the rest of a year at the beach; it is not care-free idleness. It is rather the deep satisfaction of doing what your life is all about, of fitting your efforts to your true character, of doing who you really are.

✢✢✢✢✢✢✢✢

In the world of halfway affirmation and compromise and fickleness, there is one fidelity. Our human loyalties, soon or late, are all ambiguous, even mother, father, wife, husband, and children. We float in and out of love and hate, trust and mistrust, faithfulness and fickleness. It is exhausting business. Jesus says, at the core of your life, at the center of your identity, trust this singular fidelity and nothing else. Do not let your commitment to life, your zeal for clear vision, your resolve to be a disciple, do not let it be eroded by compromise, cynicism, or despair, by imagining that the faithfulness of God can make alliances with all the "perhaps" around us. Don't split little pieces of your life away from this singular loyal love.

✢✢✢✢✢✢✢✢

Eat, enjoy, be full enough, forget enough, until we arrive at a place where we no longer say, "This do in remembrance of me," because the "me" of God has been overwhelmed in a vacuum.

✢✢✢✢✢✢✢✢

Fidelity disappears in a large binge of self-indulgence. We no longer remember the faithful God; we no longer remember to imitate God in faithfulness; we no longer remember that fidelity is the coin of humanness. Where memory fails before amnesia and where fidelity gives way to self-indulgence, in that world there will be no thanks, no acknowledgment that life is a gift; we are free to imagine it to be an achievement or a possession. Where there is no gratitude, there will be no thank-offering, no giving of self, no Eucharist, that great meal of thanks.

⚜⚜⚜⚜⚜⚜⚜⚜

The issue is not, were you comfortable? The issue is, did you do anything or learn anything about the church or about yourself, that made you uncomfortable? Did you move beyond your self-assurance and find yourself dismantled and in exile? And did you submit to the caring of mother God who comforted you beyond all your capacity to cope? Against our stern moral urgency, there is an embrace that is done at the core of our need and our hunger. Against our eager orthodoxy here is love which remembers that we are dust. It is a deep friendliness known only in displacement. And this embrace from the God who cares for exiles is the only source of support and sustenance that will be adequate for ministry, or for faith.

Chapter Five

Jesus

Jesus is beyond all usual categories of power, because he embodies the gentle, gracious, resilient, demanding power of God. He does not trifle in temples and cities and dynasties, but in the power and truth of the creator God.

⚜⚜⚜⚜⚜⚜⚜

Jesus turns everything upside down. The ones who ought to know and press to know and pretend to know have things hidden from them. And the ones who do not struggle to collect all the secrets, they have God's truth easily given to them. So, says Jesus, if you want to know the mysteries, you have been looking in the wrong place, for the little ones are the ones who know.

⚜⚜⚜⚜⚜⚜⚜

In the midst of our quest for orthodoxy to be sure people believe right, or our quest for morality to be sure people act right, or our quest for piety to be sure people pray right, the little ones know, this Jesus is enough. It is enough to know Jesus, for in Jesus you see the way God is and the way God acts. It boils down, for this Jesus, to neighbor acts and caring. For that is what Jesus did. It boils down to receiving our life from God as a gift and living it out in gratitude. If you focus on this Jesus, you will know the mystery of how life works. It will be disclosed to you, and you will have enough to live well and free and responsibly. Thus the first conversation of Jesus, the one with God, is a statement about the right rootage of faith, which cuts through all our complexity. To be with God means to stay very close to the simple, caring, demanding ways of Jesus.

⚜⚜⚜⚜⚜⚜⚜⚜

We have made Jesus too pious, too nice, too patient, too polite. He was none of these. He was a dangerous alternative kind of power that was prepared to name names and call a spade a spade, to describe social relations exactly as they were, who counted on the fact that in the end, all the raw, abusive power in the world could not prevail. His honesty is grounded in his confidence about the rule of God.

⚜⚜⚜⚜⚜⚜⚜⚜

It is exactly in Jesus, only in the Lord, that the full holiness of God has touched down in human life. The point is so obvious, and so easily forgotten. The church keeps its faith by remembering the decisiveness of Jesus.

⚜⚜⚜⚜⚜⚜⚜⚜

The church must endlessly tell its Jesus stories, because in these Jesus stories, we behold the glory of the Father, full of grace and truth. The imposition of holiness does not happen in large, grand, religious, magnificent ways. It happens where a son is welcomed home, where a neighbor is honored and cared for, where a whore is loved, where a leper is touched and cleansed, where a crowd is fed, where a guilty man is forgiven, where a crippled woman stands up straight and laughs and dances. The claim about the glory of God in the life of Jesus is not mystical, supernatural voodoo, but it is the confidence of the church that in the life of Jesus, we see all that God intends and wants and acts and asks of us. It is so daily, so concrete, so engaged with hurt, so self-giving. It is the face of this one that dazzles with life-giving light and power.

⚜⚜⚜⚜⚜⚜⚜

People wondered about Jesus. They sent and asked if he was the one who is to come, the one to be in charge. He refused a direct answer. He said, everywhere I go, true, best creation appears. The blind see, the lame walk, the lepers are cleansed, the dead are raised, the poor have their debts cancelled. Where there is a true Lord, there is a true world. Where there is a true governance, life takes on health. The governance of this God is good news, to be believed, and then to be lived!

⚜⚜⚜⚜⚜⚜⚜

We must speak about death, not because we are excessively fascinated by it or because it is fun to talk about, but because in that Friday drama, Jesus knew who he was and gave himself in love for the sake of the world, gave himself to the poor, the needy, the despairing, but also for the wise, the strong, the controlling. And in his act of vulnerability, his power to love broke all the power of violence and brutality.

⚜⚜⚜⚜⚜⚜⚜

We do not often think of Jesus as strong. But Paul has written that the weakness of Christ is stronger than

human strength. Jesus would not give in. He would not
compromise his vision or his vocation. He would not be
talked out of it by his opponents, nor by the threat of the
court, nor by the suffering of the cross. He had a quiet,
confident strength because he always knew who he was,
one with the Father. And those who follow him closely
know that kind of strength, not violent strength, but
compassionate, generous strength, the capacity to be in
the world differently, and so occupied with the newness
of the world.

❧❧❧❧❧❧❧❧❧

There is an insistence in the life of Jesus, that innocence
gives power, that inhumanity is not a safe policy, that
honesty is required of reality, and things must be called
by their right names. It matters enormously if power disputes are in the context of unaccommodating moral reality. Jesus got himself killed because he exposed the false
ordering of power that paid no attention to the little ones,
among whom he counted himself.

❧❧❧❧❧❧❧❧❧

Jesus has become for us the lens through which we
reread power, social relations, and formal policies. Jesus
stands alongside all the powerless in his abrasive prayer,
demanding justice on earth from God. Jesus' innocence is an exposé of and a threat to every other kind of
power. It would indeed be quite an Easter if the church
resolved to come clean on this moral claim. Talk about
a coup! No wonder he made the governor nervous and
the crowd frantic. They killed him, but he kept praying in his dangerous, abrasive honesty. The prayer he
prays insists that God will not be mocked, "For the LORD

hears the needy, and does not despise his own that are in bonds" (Ps. 69:33).

✤✤✤✤✤✤✤✤

Jesus was a deep disruption wherever he went. Jesus was a misfit; he did not fit anybody's categories. Jesus was weird and they did not know what to do with him. When he entered the room, everything changed. Wherever he sat immediately, promptly became the head of the table.

✤✤✤✤✤✤✤✤

In a world of fear and alienation and resentment and grudge and anxiety, Jesus comes to be a peacemaker. Such peace as he can make happens only through vulnerability, being exposed to risk, and so breaking the vicious cycles of violence. The reference to his "blood" is a way of speaking about his suffering love wherein he deals with the power of death that surrounds us. The world of Jesus is different. It is a world where he has made peace. And we now who are baptized are welcomed into his company and his work to be peacemakers in hard places, to refuse the way of anger and fear and hate and resentment, in order to enact a world of gratitude, generosity, and forgiveness.

✤✤✤✤✤✤✤✤

The people heard Jesus say to Zacchaeus, "You are a son of Abraham." Jesus said to the tax collector, the old life-giving promises of Genesis apply to you and count for you, and you have a future because God has made promises to you. The ordinary people had never heard such talk or been permitted to think such a thing. They had never heard of a God who made promises that gave futures. And they had certainly never heard it said to them. For the managers of the status quo had monopolized all the good news and all the old stories and all the live promises for themselves, and had left ordinary people on the outside, not even looking in. They were spellbound, because they did not think such a thing was possible. They rejoiced and gathered around him.

They not only heard and were spellbound. They watched and were spellbound. What they saw is that this strange man not only talked the talk. He walked the walk among them. His person carried power to heal and transform and make new. They saw it, the ones who had no access to healing and no entry to forgiveness. They had been shut out and he let them in. They already sensed, as he had told John the Baptist: Everywhere I go, the power of new life swirls around . . . the blind see, the lame walk, the deaf hear, lepers are cleansed, the dead are raised, the poor rejoice. Gathered in a spellbinding cluster were the former blind, the former poor, the former deaf, the former lame, the former dead, the former lepers, all "former," all now made insiders. And the old insiders resisted the loss of monopoly. You could not stay neutral about Jesus; you either opposed him, or you committed to him.

⚜⚜⚜⚜⚜⚜⚜

The test and norm is the reality of Jesus. Look at Jesus, because Jesus confronts all the throne talk of the world. You want to know about joy, and well-being, and truth, and goodness. Look at Jesus. Not being served, but serving. I have no doubt that the world depends on Jesus. I have no doubt that on a day-to-day basis, the world depends on the Jesus people who give their lives. What else would you do but give your life? Would you keep and save your life and let it grow sour? No, give it as a ransom. Think this day about being in another conversation, another community, another cup, another baptism. We are at a crucial moment in our society. In this moment, we are given a glimpse of a more excellent way. Local churches, local conversations, local servanthood, local giving, local cups to drink, local baptisms to live, local ways of being faithful and joyous, local ways of power for life. The story in Mark 10:35–45 begins with greedy thrones. By the end of the story, the subject is changed. Now the subject is servanthood and healing and ransom. What a way to be first and great! Come and have your subject changed.

❧❧❧❧❧❧❧❧

From the beginning, we have known this about Jesus, full of grace and truth. We have known his stories and have remembered his flesh. But from the beginning we have known one other astonishing truth about Jesus. We have known, as the church has always known, that Jesus is part of a larger story. No, not a part of the bigger story, but the center and focus and lead character of the big story of heaven and earth. Since its first utterance the church has worked, as well as it could, to connect this Nazareth guy—born of Mary, executed by Rome—to the great mystery of the world. We have not been able to say everything we sensed about him. Some of our attempts to say it have been silly, a little primitive, embarrassingly supernatural, but we have kept trying in the church because we have not wanted to let the story of Jesus be a small story that flattens his mystery, or denies his glow, or limits his power for newness.

❧❧❧❧❧❧❧❧

This is what we have seen in the guy from Nazareth. This is the cloud rider of whom we sing in doxology. This is

the one who calls to obedience, away from all our commitments to death. We may rejoice in our vocation, for
we—after Jesus—are situated in sync with the truth of
the world. Imagine holy truth—aligned with widows and
orphans and prisoners and the homeless. No wonder it
is good news. The good news is that the link between
heaven and earth is not broken. It still pertains. That is
what we say when we confess, He ascended into heaven
and is seated on the right hand of God the Father. Good
news indeed!

❧❧❧❧❧❧❧❧❧

Coming to church is so routine, so predictable, so often
boring and nothing, jaded against the odd claim that in
Jesus of Nazareth has come the odd God of Sinai with
new command. We were not there, but the purpose of the
story in its reading is to let us hear and reenter the narrative, to know the same fear of holy intrusion, to hear the
same words, "Do not fear," that gives us access to Jesus.
And then to look again and see only Jesus. That is all there
was. That is all there is. That is all our faith is about.

Chapter Six

Justice

The song of Israel opens for us another side of the God who reigns in power. It turns out that God's reign is not simply about power. It is about a relationship of caring fidelity, wherein God is in solidarity with the most vulnerable and most needy in society, which in ancient Israel includes

- orphans who lack a protector in a patriarchal society, so that God is a father for those who have no father;
- widows who lack a male protector in a patriarchal society, so that this God is a protector of the unprotected;
- prisoners who, then as now, were characteristically poor people who lacked resources or a smart lawyer. Thus God is an ally to those whom society would hold in bondage.

It turns out that the one who has ascended into power is not transcendent in remoteness, is not splendid in indifference, but is deeply in touch with the reality of the earth where money and power and social leverage and differentiation of gender, race, and class leave some dangerously exposed. This father-God to whom we pray "our father" rides the clouds not as a joy rider, but rather to be in a position to see and to know and to care and to intervene and to feed and to heal and to forgive and to reconcile and to liberate. It turns out that ascension, whereby God is celebrated in power, is a claim that the earth is ordered differently because of the one who governs it.

✤✤✤✤✤✤✤✤✤

Jesus urges his disciples to be interruptive servants of God, filing claims, seeking justice, crying out day and night, so that the space in the heavenly court is occupied and redefined by appeals for transformative, restorative justice.

✤✤✤✤✤✤✤✤✤

Forgiveness is first of all an economic transaction and the big forgiveness concerns debts. We now live in an indebted society. The ownership class keeps all the others in hock, and the poor live in helpless poverty in third-class status with poor schools and poor health care. And the children suffer more. And we are sent, by Jesus, to break the vicious cycles of debt and to restore folk to full societal participation, by charity, by attentive neighborliness, and by policy. This is the most radical thing the church can do, as it was the most radical thing that Jesus did. The church can be active in breaking the various patterns of debt and the hopeless attitudes of resentment toward the poor and the lethal assumption that if you are on top, you deserve it, and let the others fall out because, who cares? Forgiveness is the recalculating of society for the participation of all of its members.

❧❧❧❧❧❧❧❧❧

The reason that Sabbath is a radical discipline is that it is a regular, disciplined, highly visible withdrawal from the acquisitive society of production and consumption that is shaped only by commodity. Work stoppage and rest are public statements that one's existence and the existence of one's society are not defined by the pursuit of commodity, and that human well-being is not evoked by commodity but precisely by the intentional refusal of commodity.

❧❧❧❧❧❧❧❧❧

We are now, in anxious America, in a contest for creation. You can call it an environmental crisis. You can call it an economic crisis. You can call it world hunger or oil spill. You can call it constitutionalism in the defense of the way it used to be. Whatever you call it, we are in contest to see if creation—awed land—can be embraced as God's good gift that evokes gratitude and not avarice. The invitation is to counter the divisive work, the violence, the excessive ownership, the seduction, the amnesia, to see the wonder of creation out beyond our consuming anxiety. The creator God knows what we need, and gives bread to the eater and seed to the sower. But, he says, such seek God's justice in the world. The force of covenant in a world of possessiveness is a hard task. It is our calling. We are always deciding how creation is, and how we shall be lead creatures for God among all the creatures. The hard work of this calling does not permit romanticism about creation.

❧❧❧❧❧❧❧❧❧

The God of the Bible is not a passive keeper of order. The God of the Bible is not a neutral referee in life's conflicts. The God of the Bible is active, intervening, and has taken sides for the poor and the needy who thought that they had no advocate.

⚜⚜⚜⚜⚜⚜

The interlocking relationship between the big-time producers who are mesmerized by production and the lowly workers who invisibly produce creates a social situation in which nobody is permitted Sabbath. In such an environment defined by the practice of acquisitiveness, all parties to the social network are caught in a context of coercion that mandates always increasing production quotas, all of which echo the old imperial demand, "Make more bricks."

⚜⚜⚜⚜⚜⚜

The demanding act of love is justice, the guarantee of a viable life for all members of the new humanity. I understand that the big justice questions are difficult and remote from us in our daily lives. But clearly the Psalmist thought big about human dominion, to take in the whole scope of the human process. It is the case, I believe, that the church must care about such issues as health care and protection of workers and prisoners, because there is no one else to stay at these urgent questions. And, therefore, the local church is an arena where the big issues of humanity receive our study and our prayer and our engagement.

⚜⚜⚜⚜⚜⚜

There is kindness, but there is also justice and righteousness, and we must take care that we do not separate these;

that we do not think we can have the one without the other; that we do not choose persons or structures, kindness or justice, because the one who liberates, also cares about, the Christ who fed the hungry and cared for the sick is also the Christ who challenged the Pharisees and the government and had to be executed because he scared too many important people.

⁕⁕⁕⁕⁕⁕⁕⁕⁕

God's creation is so fragile and tenuous and precarious. It depends upon God's fidelity that in turn requires human fidelity to care for the earth. And when that care of the earth fails, the infrastructure of the whole fails. Because the world is not a closed system, not a fixed structure, not "nature." It is God's creation that is ordered and loved by God. And it is put at risk by human carelessness and arrogance.

⁕⁕⁕⁕⁕⁕⁕⁕⁕

Jesus makes a contrast between present wealth that you cannot keep anyway, because it will be gone, and future home that is an eternal realm in God's presence. You see, Jesus is talking about money and through money and beyond money, to get his disciples to think differently about their future. When you get caught up in the economy, you can only think about taxes and capital gains and 401(k)s and growth stocks and mortgages and accumulation and credits. That is the horizon of our global economy and we are swept up in it, as all the money whirls around us.

But, says Jesus, that is no real horizon for anything. That is just short term, present tense. Beyond the short-term present tense, there is more. There is growing old and growing older and dying and being remembered and being treasured and being loved and being cared for and being welcomed into the truth of God's own life.

❧❧❧❧❧❧❧❧❧

I submit that the experience of exile-displacement-deportation and the counteraction of gathering offer an apt characterization of the process of ministry among us. This double motif refers, in our context, to the fact that all the conventional, homegrown props of established society are now largely gone. Old institutions scarcely perform their tasks anymore, and that reality of loss generates enormous, amorphous anxiety among us. Thus, I propose that the church is now God's agent for gathering exiles of which I can think immediately of two groups. First, there are those exiles who have been made exiles by the force of our society, those who are rejected, ostracized, and labeled as outsiders. This, of course, includes the poor, and inevitably we would also think in one way or another of gays and lesbians. We have an exile-producing culture that displaces some folk who are variously visible and vocal among us. But second, after the obviously excluded, I suggest that the category of "exile" also includes those whom the world may judge normal, conventional, establishment types. For the truth is that the large failure of old values and old institutions causes many people to experience themselves as displaced people . . . anxious, under threat, vigilant, ill at ease, and so in pursuit of safety and stability and well-being that is not on the horizons of contemporary society. It is not obvious among us how the dream of well-being can come to fruition among us.

❧❧❧❧❧❧❧❧❧

It is the truth itself that is in jeopardy among us, the truth that God intends the transformation of the world into a community, the truth that God intends haves and have-nots to be in it together, the truth that the outsiders of the world are insiders to God's regime, the truth that hospitality as a social strategy is more adequate than vengeance: all of this is at risk in a society that does not notice and that does not pay attention.

✤✤✤✤✤✤✤✤✤✤

The church is deeply committed to the practice of neighborly justice that knows that God peculiarly loves the devalued, the marginal, and the unproductive. I talk about this because the church quarrels about the issue and never quite gets clear that God cares about the healing of the world in its economic, political, and social dimensions.

✤✤✤✤✤✤✤✤✤✤

This is perhaps the most radical teaching in the Bible, that the haves are bound in neighborliness to the have-nots. Of course, this is charity and we all believe in charity. Except that Deuteronomy is law, and this is social policy. This is a welfare program that modestly redistributes resources in order that all may live. Of course, the world cares not at all for aliens and widows and orphans who are a social hazard and a public inconvenience, or refugees or criminals, or welfare mothers or the landless or the vulnerable. But the story of the Bible is so written that God's care for the disenfranchised is a main theme, mostly screened out by those who like to talk a lot about biblical authority. It is as though Jesus starts every meeting by asking, "Are there any here with withered hands, any widows, any orphans, any aliens, any lepers, any blind, any poor, any homeless? Come forward and be the focus of healing attention."

✤✤✤✤✤✤✤✤✤✤

The reality of the poor does not need verification. They are among us, and their number grows. And the reality of the poor does not need argument among us. We not only acknowledge that reality in which we are implicated. We also affirm together that the reality of the poor, real as it is, is not a fixed fate. Things can and will be changed. So we are here as an act of hope. So I speak to you not about the reality which is our premise, but about our sure hope that it need not be so, and about the sure resolve of God that it will not be so. The reality of the poor is not a given in human history. It is a momentary contrivance. It is a contrivance done with such care and power and resilience that it is formidable. But it is nonetheless a momentary contrivance.

The great claim of biblical faith is that this contrivance cannot withstand the resolve of God and cannot withstand the obedient imaginative caring of God's people. One does not have to be cynical to say that the resolve of God is a much more reliable basis than the care of God's people, but both matter. We are not here because we are fatigued, though some of us are, or in despair, though some of us are close to that, but because we hope and trust and believe for a newness that is sure to come and for which we wait. It is an important theological and intellectual gain for us if we even agree, against our own vested interest, that the poor are a contrivance in the world and not a given, no matter how habitual it all seems.

❧❧❧❧❧❧❧❧❧

The God who governs the gods is not a vacuous, generic ruler. Rather this God stands by the codes of neighborliness upon which the world depends. This God takes no bribes, which means is not aligned with the rich and the powerful. This God knows the Jewish triad that is nearly a mantra: "widow, orphan, sojourner." This God, right from the vision of a heavenly throne, is the one who collects the food, who runs clothing drives, who cares about justice of an economic sort.

It's about the deep, nonnegotiable commitment this God makes without regard to nationality, creed, race, or sexual preference; it's about food and clothing and health care and education and all the dimensions of human community that are grounded in the God of all neighbors.

⚜⚜⚜⚜⚜⚜

It always remains one more time for the church to decide how deeply it will go into servanthood. And we enter it at many different levels. But what is clear is that there is no covenant without cost. There is no homecoming without somebody being bruised in the process. The prisoners are not set free and the world is not redefined without risky intervention.

⚜⚜⚜⚜⚜⚜

Ministry cannot be about maintenance; it is about gathering, about embrace, about welcoming home "all sorts and conditions" of people. Home is a place for the mother tongue, of basic soul food, of old stories told and treasured, of being at ease, known by name, belonging without qualifying for membership. The ministry of gathering is one to which this God has been committed forever. I have no doubt, moreover, that gathering is now a crucial ministry not only among the visibly excluded but among the visibly included who nonetheless know themselves to be marginated and increasingly powerless and under threat.

⚜⚜⚜⚜⚜⚜

Imagine a church of Word and sacrament making claims,

- that exile is a choosable venue for life as alternative to a safe, ordered coherence that is at most an ideological construct;
- that others belong with us and for us and are welcome as we are welcomed, an alternative so much more healthy than urging exclusivism or pretending that the others are not there;
- that generosity to the neighbor creates futures that self-indulgent acquisitiveness can never offer;
- that Sabbath disengagement from production causes us not to fall behind but to redeem our lives from the frantic rat race; and
- that yielding and relinquishing in prayer is a proper human mode given the Holy One who loves us.

⚜⚜⚜⚜⚜⚜⚜

The truth about us—enacted in Jesus—is that the hostility, fear, competition is over. The strangers are welcomed home, the sojourners are made citizens, the aliens now belong. The reality of peace is asserted in the face of our endless illusions about not belonging. Think of it today, you in your arrogance, or you in your defeat. Belonging matters, and you must decide how you will deal with your membership in this community where God governs.

⚜⚜⚜⚜⚜⚜⚜

The claim of success and security, so powerful among us, causes us not to notice the cast out and often not to acknowledge our own displacement or anxiety about coming displacement. Openness to foreigners and eunuchs, that is, welcome to others who are not like us, is a radical alternative to the ideology of conformity that takes all those not like ourselves to be dangerous and unacceptable deviants. The issue, of course, concerns the otherness of sexuality, but it also concerns the otherness of immigrants and those with alternative social practices. And here is this poet who says, let not the foreigner or the eunuch imagine that they will be excluded or forgotten.

The memory of the exodus that leads to neighborly generosity is the primary mark of a covenantal society. That memory in practice issues in a subordination of the economy to the social fabric with focal attention to the marginated who are without social access, social power, or social advocacy. The covenant is an assertion of interdependence and an institution of mutuality that flies in the face of acquisitiveness that regards everyone else as a competitor for the same commodity or as a threat to my self-securing. The poem is an act of imagination that allows that social relationships are not necessarily cast in terms of aggressive commodity competition, for there is a more elemental belonging with and for each other that chastens such aggressiveness.

⚜⚜⚜⚜⚜⚜⚜

It's not about capitalism or socialism; it's about being human in another, gospel way.

⚜⚜⚜⚜⚜⚜⚜

Jesus is not an economist. I am not an economist. But he has in his horizon long-term economics, long-term neighborliness, long-term forgiveness, long-term friendship, long-term welcome, long-term neighborliness with God to all eternity. This is not liberal or conservative, not Democrat or Republican. It is the truth of the gospel.

Chapter Seven

Evangelical Identity

The hallmark of the church is not certitude; it is openness to the Spirit.

❧❧❧❧❧❧❧❧

One task of the church is, of course, advocacy of this alternative testimony to the coming rule of God and the profound regime change entertained in this new governance. But advocacy by itself is inadequate. Therefore, I propose that the church be a safe venue for the hosting of ambiguity about these options that may be named and identified. Most of us are exceedingly complex and ambivalent about the great issues. Dominant society wants not to honor that complexity, and so we are accustomed to many layers of denial. In our various arenas of denial, God's spirit has little chance for newness. The first break in our common denial is to give voice to ambiguity and thereby to have an awareness that alternatives are indeed available and choosable.

❧❧❧❧❧❧❧❧

The Friday people of pain have never given in to immobilizing anxiety, but have told the truth that makes free. The Sunday people of hope have never given in to despair, but have always known that newness breaks fresh from the word fleshed and then words on our lips.

❧❧❧❧❧❧❧❧❧

We can tell the stories of Elisha, Jesus, and Peter and John, the stories of the boy and the little girl and the blind beggar. There are more stories; these we have considered are not the final stories. There is a fourth story; and we are to enact it. We are to act in it because we stand in the stream of this narrative truth. We are empowered for the disabled. We are given resources for resurrection capacities. We discover in our own tired bones capacity to heal and empower others. And we, along with them, are invited to dancing and jumping and leaping and singing and praising God. Because Jesus is the Lord of the dance; Jesus is the leader of the jump; Jesus is the voice of our singing. The fourth story, our story of faith, goes with the other three, enacted today and soon and often, and then later told to our children.

❧❧❧❧❧❧❧❧❧

So ponder this. You are sent to forgive. You are sent to be a cottage industry in forgiveness. It is the church's primary assignment from the Easter Christ to forgive.

❧❧❧❧❧❧❧❧❧

It is clear that the church needs no more custodians to keep it running the way it has been. It now needs no more pastors or leaders who will conduct business as usual. Because we are in an emergency situation in our society where the gospel matters decisively. What the church now requires "by faith," I suggest,

- is to run risks for justice in a brutalizing society;
- is to run risks for forgiveness in a vengeful society;
- is to run risks for hospitality in an exclusionary society;
- is to run risks for generosity in a parsimonious society;
- is to run risks for the scandal of Easter resurrection in a society that reduces everything to our reasonable possibilities;
- is to run risks for poetic imagination in a society of prosaic anxiety.

⚜⚜⚜⚜⚜⚜⚜⚜⚜

The intention of God is to create a community of holy people—not goody-goody people, but people who look like the God we have come to know in Jesus.

⚜⚜⚜⚜⚜⚜⚜⚜⚜

The great fact in the life of the church today is not ecumenicity nor renewal nor small groups nor coffeehouses nor any of the things about which we might like to think. The great fact in the life of the church today is conflict, the failure of communication and the posture of mistrust which permeates church life in every dimension. This is almost amusing if it were not so sad, that this people charged with reconciliation, entrusted with a message of good news, should be so torn. And that would not be undesirable, if we did not have to add another observation: it is conflict which we seem not to be able to handle in creative or constructive ways. One can give it many names: of clergy vs. laity, of conservatives vs. liberals, of local people against the bureaucrats. All these point, I think, to an issue that is peculiarly alive in our time; the question of whether or not the church shall be engaged in its mission. We seem to divide most over the question of what the church shall do and be. Some think the job of the church is to maintain a spiritual oasis where persons can, from time to time, be refreshed and renewed, away from the strain and tension of the world. Others think the church must be an agent of social and cultural change; not a place of refreshing retreat, but an actor in the midst of the struggle. And on this each of us has strong feelings; so strong that the life and ministry of the church is less effective.

❧❧❧❧❧❧❧❧

This moment of crisis in the church is a moment to consider among us the richness of the treasure and the fragility of the vessel in the presence of the treasure. It may be a moment to decide yet again to give ourselves over to the truth of the treasure and let God manage much of the rest for the sake of the vessel.

We are watching while the clay pots are being smashed like Jeremiah imagined old Jerusalem to be smashed, smashed maybe for being disobedient and irrelevant, smashed for being too self-preoccupied, smashed for being too comfortable with privilege and national ideology and middle-class morality. So I had the thought, the clay pots are being smashed for the sake of Jesus, that the power of Jesus in his generosity, forgiveness, hospitality, and justice can break loose in the world to make for healing and newness.

❧❧❧❧❧❧❧❧

We have this ministry, not because God is heavy-handed, or authoritarian or self-serving, but by God's mercy. It is a gift given by God. It is because of God's gentle, caring, engaged, compassionate purpose with us, that ministry becomes a mode of being oddly human in the world. Ministry is never easy, because the world is resistant and dismissive. It is not easy in a world of brutality and greed and ambition. But Paul says, "We do not lose heart." We will not be talked out of our identity and our purpose, our vocation and our vision. We do not lose heart because the work is rooted in God's own holiness and driven by God's own spirit, and there is enough in that to keep to this odd purpose.

⚜⚜⚜⚜⚜⚜⚜⚜

We are baptized, given a different cup. What an image, set down in every community where we live, there is a church planting, a place where people come regularly to talk differently about cups and baptisms and servanthood and new kinds of power that the world cannot understand. It is this community in every place who hold to another way in the world, because we have a glimpse of a cup that runs over with joy and peace and mercy and well-being. That, of course, depends on our accepting that we are different, and in the world for a different purpose.

⚜⚜⚜⚜⚜⚜⚜⚜

In my judgment, we must now face hard decisions such as we have not faced for a long time. We have indeed bought in as individual persons, even as church, on consumerism, aimed at self-indulgence, comfort, security, and safety. We live our lives out of our affluence, and we discover that all our self-indulgence makes us satiated but neither happy nor safe.

This US propensity, moreover, is supported by militarism, by strength, muscle, and intimidation, so that our culture, its images and its rhetoric, are saturated with military pictures bespeaking violence and brutality, and none of it makes us safe. It is like being taken in by the values of the Babylonian empire, with its lush dreams of war and promises of prosperity.

But none of that is for Israel, so says the poet. None of it is for the church. None of it is our proper way in the world. So the poet holds out to the exiles (and to us) an alternative way, the waters of baptism, the bread of the Eucharist, the wine of new covenant, the capacity to risk and trust and obey, and then to find ourselves safe and joyous, close to God, and enlisted for a very different life in the world.

❖❖❖❖❖❖❖❖❖

Holiness erupts and glows. Holiness transforms and makes us new. Holiness becomes mercy for ministry.

❖❖❖❖❖❖❖❖❖

There is one baptism. All of us as adult Christians and most of us as young have been baptized. But have we considered what this means? In that dramatic moment, we receive a name, an identity, a worth. In my tradition we practice infant baptism, because we insist that we do not choose our name or earn it or deserve it. It is given us in love. We don't pick the name, but the name guarantees us. Now that is a great thing in a world of computers and impersonality. Nobody can take that name from us. Nobody can touch our identity. Nobody can finally question our worth. We know who we are, and in the fellowship, we know who our brother is. Much of the threat felt by people today is in this loss of identity and therefore their sense of worth. Often because we do not believe our name, we do not know our identity, we doubt our worth, often we choose conflict and hostility. Often when unsure of self we are unable to put off our old nature because there we find our security. Often we are not able to put on our new nature because we can't stand the threat. Baptism is that dramatic symbol that guarantees our security so that we are free to mature.

⚜⚜⚜⚜⚜⚜⚜⚜

Ours is a particularly narcissistic age in which we are pre-occupied with self, with appearance, with style, with security or, as my preacher said, "I may not be much, but I am all I ever think about."

Not so! You do not, says the catechism, belong to yourself. You do not belong to the rat race of the consumer economy. You do not belong to the national security state with its aggressive militarism. You do not belong to the culture of greed and selfishness and violence and indifference. That is not who you are. Rather, you belong to, rely upon, and answer to Jesus Christ. That is what our baptism and our confirmation is about, and why we meet regularly, so that we are not talked out of our identity.

⚜⚜⚜⚜⚜⚜⚜⚜

The mission to which we are called is the reordering of all of life according to the categories of vulnerability, solidarity, and fidelity. So the issue is not simply to practice covenanting among ourselves, but to be the agent, catalyst, offer of covenant with the world that waits for good news.

⚜⚜⚜⚜⚜⚜⚜⚜

So this is a community that has as its agenda, to break with patterns of falseness and pretense, to become persons and community at ease with risk, at joy in generosity, at peace with neighbors unlike ourselves who have gifts to give us. Remember, we are the ones who rely on broken bread and do not need to own the bakery. We are the ones who trust poured-out wine, even if we do not monopolize the vincyards.

⚜⚜⚜⚜⚜⚜

If it is right that we live in a time when we are rendered small and insignificant and powerless, then I suggest that it is the work of pastor and church to counter such minimizing of humankind by a celebration, appreciation, and affirmation of humankind and human persons. The church is called to stand against human diminishment, and to live and to act and speak in ways that enhance human persons in human community. The Psalm says, "What is man?" And the answer is, human persons are the ultimate creatures of all creation. So let the church stand in this place for the full celebration of humanity, as a counter to the mean, angry, cheap ways in which the world dismisses human persons as cheap labor, as cannon fodder, as replaceable parts, as mindless objects of propaganda and advertising. Let it be that every person who touches the church is magnified and celebrated and affirmed according to the glory of God.

⚜⚜⚜⚜⚜⚜

If the church in America is to recover energy for mission, it requires being clear on who God is, because our understanding of God has become soft and fuzzy and romantic and compromised.

⚜⚜⚜⚜⚜⚜

The purpose of the sentinel, that is the whole people, is to keep reminding God of God's unfinished business. That is the vocation of God's people as sentinel . . . to hound God and nag God and hold God to God's promises. What an amazing vocation for God's people: To remind God of God's own commitments; to insist that the task must be finished by God; to offer endless petitions to God, bearing witness to the world. . . . The people of God are to expect more and to insist upon more, and to watch to make sure it happens. God has promised, but the promise depends in part upon the powerful, persistent petitions and the nervy nagging of God's people.

❧❧❧❧❧❧❧❧

Blessed is the church that does not easily come to terms with the present, that keeps loose and open enough, restless enough to know that the present arrangements of reality are not good enough, and they are not the way God intends them.

❧❧❧❧❧❧❧❧

There is a mistaken noncovenantal notion about the church floating around. And it is like a disease. It is that we are all Christians, or all believers, or at least all well-intentioned people. And thus we all come together to cooperate as best we can. This is called a "voluntary association" of like-minded people who choose a mission together and stay at it as long as we choose.

But let us be clear, that is not the church that is offered in the Bible. To speak of a "voluntary association" may be an accurate statement of sociology, but the Bible makes its claims on other grounds. The church of the Bible is not a voluntary association of people who stay together because it is convenient to do so. In the Bible, the church is not our idea or our invention. It is God's idea. As we say in our Statement of Faith, "God calls us into the church" for the sake of the mission. We are bound together, not because we agree or like each other or feel comfortable, but because there is a call from God and to each other. And that means we have a right to expect something special of each other and of ourselves. What we have a right to expect is that people will respond to the call of God even when it does not suit. Often God's call to mission is in tension with our preferences, with our vested interests. Our business is to call each other to act against our preferences and against our vested interests. And therefore in quite concrete ways, on budgets and programs, we have always to be asking about God's call that likely suits none of our vested interests.

❦❦❦❦❦❦❦❦❦

Jesus is filled with healing power. He keeps doing these strange wonders of restoration. The business of Jesus is to restore people to full social participation and to insist that the main business of the church is to do the same thing Jesus does, to restore the disabled to full social existence. That's us! That's what we do!

❦❦❦❦❦❦❦❦❦

The church is to be odd in the world, noticed in the community for walking to a different drummer. What Jesus intends is that the church should share in the suffering of Jesus . . . because Jesus' way in the world is not popular or safe.

❦❦❦❦❦❦❦❦❦

The church is not called to pious, romantic, goosey religion, but simply to practice the memory of Jesus, and to let that memory be fully present tense. When that story of Jesus is present tense, we are able to sort out and identify all the empty claims where God's holiness and God's power for life does not reside, where God's power for life is not embodied or enacted. Christians sort these matters out around Jesus, because we are endlessly seduced by imagining the glory is to be found in our technology, in our brightness, in our achievement, in our power, in our wealth, in our loveliness, or in our fitness. No, no, no! But in the face and body and life and story of the one who suffers in and with and for the world. Holiness in its decisive form is suffering that heals.

⚜⚜⚜⚜⚜⚜⚜⚜⚜

You see, the Bible asserts that this coming of God's holiness is what and how God chooses to act. But the Bible also asserts that this coming of God's holiness is the deepest yearning and the most powerful craving that we have. We are born and created and formed by God to want to be with God and in God's presence. We are made for God's holiness, and it is exactly God's holiness that makes us human. It is the glory of God and the wonder of God that make our life joyously whole. That is the truth about us.

⚜⚜⚜⚜⚜⚜⚜⚜⚜

The church consists in those who have taken as their life's work the staggering possibility of growing congenial to and reflective of God's own life. But the crucial news of this staggering possibility is not that we have this hard work to do. The news is that God is at work and we are being transformed, being acted upon, being addressed, cared for, suffered over, bothered with by the very power and purpose of God.

❖❖❖❖❖❖❖❖

Ministry seems so odd, so marginal to our life, so institutional, so much for somebody else. It is not any of these. Ministry is the day-to-day human work of bringing more and more of our life under the joy and purpose and power of God. It is not an extra or an add-on. It is not an elective for the second Saturday of the spring term, but it is a way of living that lets the transformative power of God operate for the sake of human dignity, social justice, healed creation, for the world beloved of God. And it is ours, yours and mine!

❖❖❖❖❖❖❖❖

I believe that we are very close to the time in American society where authentic Christianity will not come easy and perhaps at a price. And the church will need to decide if it will simply be an echo of the great voices of fear and repression or if it is prepared to take a quite different stance because of its faith and the call of its Lord.

❖❖❖❖❖❖❖❖

The whole church, not just the twelve apostles, is in the business of testimony to the truth of Easter. That is what the church is about, to give testimony by act and by speech and by policy and by prayer, that the future is open to life, because death cannot win.

❖❖❖❖❖❖❖❖

The time is coming for the church when we shall have to decide if we do indeed believe God is God, if we will put our lives where our mouths are. And the issue is a simple one. Either God is Lord and so we are safe and free to serve him, or he is not Lord and so we must live in fear and defensiveness, and that issue, when it comes, cannot be ducked.

❧❧❧❧❧❧❧❧❧

The church is not a group of people bent on self-help or well-being or even transformation, even metamorphosis. It is rather a community whose very life consists in ministry. God's holiness does not come among us for purposes of pious masturbation. God's holiness is given, to Moses, to Jesus, even to us, in order to be engaged in the very large work that belongs to our true identity.

❧❧❧❧❧❧❧❧❧

The story of the Bible is God's work of finding and naming and uttering and sending a small community as an antidote to the dysfunction of the world.

❧❧❧❧❧❧❧❧❧

The Bible is the long story of those discomforted by ministry: Moses, Jeremiah, Ezra, Peter, Paul, Stephen. . . . It is not different with Luther and Calvin and Barth and Nouwen and Solle and Sider and Wallis . . . all models for us, and we notice that they are not comfortable in ministry. Or conversely, you will look a long time in the Bible for anyone called of God who is "comfortable." Indeed, a comfortable ministry is something of an oxymoron.

❧❧❧❧❧❧❧❧❧

In Judaism, the eleventh commandment is "Thou shalt not forget." And we Christians regularly say, in our most precious act, "As often as you do it, do it in remembrance of me." We Christians, like Jews, are big on remembrance. We are set deep in a particular memory that tells us who we are and what we must do. And yet, for the most part, we live in a culture that forgets, and even the church suffers a great deal from amnesia. It is my judgment that the recovery of our very peculiar memory is an urgent project in the church, one necessary to the faithfulness and vitality of the church.

⚜⚜⚜⚜⚜⚜⚜⚜

What causes a community to forget its most treasured past? Why would a community let the children forget its most precious account of its own life? The answers are easy enough to identify:

- being safe and affluent, so that the memories of dependence and need and rescue and transformation are no longer relevant and seem remote;
- being so impressed with the present that the past seems shabby, if not embarrassing. Scholars now say we are seeing a "thinning" of our past, because of things, consumerism, fast communication, any long-term commitment that is not fully in the NOW;
- being so much the center of reality, so full of self, so dazzled by wealth and power that telling stories about another time, another place, another Agent is just plain old slow and boring.

⚜⚜⚜⚜⚜⚜⚜⚜

Children devalue memory only because the parents devalue memory. It is not that the children are indifferent; it is that they get the clear, unmistakable message from the parents that none of this matters. And so everything for parents is busy and fast, instantaneous and quick, and throwaway. And soon there is no moral habitat, no imaginative environment, no set of signals and code phrases that give us rootage and belonging; and we are on our own, perhaps glad to be, perhaps frightened of it, but either way, with no one but us.

Chapter Eight

Neighbor Love

It is now an urgent season for neighborliness that will contradict our consumerism, that will subvert our inordinate militarism, and that will refuse the culture of appearance. We have other things to do with our lives in our God-given freedom.

⚜⚜⚜⚜⚜⚜

The key act of love is forgiveness. We know how it is in churches, especially rural churches, and in families of all kind. We get crossways and we cannot let it go. We keep a grudge forever and we recruit our children into the grudge, and never forget the day we were wounded or offended. But human persons, in all of their God-given majesty, can break the vicious cycle of grudge and forgive and begin again. That is what the new commandment permits.

⚜⚜⚜⚜⚜⚜

The juxtaposition of "hospitality" and "vengeance" is telling. Vengeance is a practice that perceives others as threat or competitor or rival; the opposite is hospitality that sees the other as guest. On the one hand, it is clear that we live in an inordinately vengeful society, and the Christian community is called to counter that propensity with hospitality. On the other hand, if we ask what makes hospitality a possible practice, I submit that hospitality is possible for those who trust their creatureliness and who are not under compulsion, that is, those who practice Sabbath. I have no doubt that Sabbath rest can indeed break the cycle of vengefulness, precisely because it breaks the pattern of drivenness that eventuates in violence against the neighbor.

⚜⚜⚜⚜⚜⚜

Jesus has given a new commandment, that we love one another. And then it is added,

> We love because he first loved us. Those who say, "I love God," and hate their brothers or sisters, are liars; for those who do not love a brother or sister whom they have seen, cannot love God whom they have not seen. The commandment we have from him is this: those who love God must love their brothers and sisters also. (1 John 4:19–21)

And Jesus went to great length to identify "sister and brother" as everyone, including those most unlike us, those who do not fit, those who upset us and make us uncomfortable.

⚜⚜⚜⚜⚜⚜

Love. What a gospel word in a society that is increasingly given over to exclusion, to hate, and to vengeance! There is an ideology at work among us that wants to make the world very small, in order to make it safe for us, and to exclude and eliminate everyone who is not like us. That attraction to hate and resentment spins off in policies concerning immigrants and capital punishment, so that our hate of the other turns to violent vengeance, and all in the name of religious piety. Such a practice of hurt that is among us is a contradiction to the father of mercy who loves all the children and protects all the weak ones.

⚜⚜⚜⚜⚜⚜⚜

There is a mistaken notion that we are self-starters, individuals who "possess" capacity and worth. And we can make do and can do, if we try harder. Such a view belongs to American notions of success and progress. But it really doesn't work. We cannot make it alone. We depend on this other one. We cannot and need not have life on our own terms. Because at the deep levels of our lives, we do not have such capacities. We are mostly a conundrum of fears and unfulfilled hopes.

We are not self-invented folks. We are always creatures of another who speaks to us and calls us by name and calls us into being. In a primary way, we are individual persons because God knows our names, and as with all creation, God calls us into being. We live by God's faithful call to us. And in a derivative way, we live by the daily call of the neighbor. We wait each day to be called by name, to be cared for, to have someone expect something of us and give something to us. And in the process we learn in many ways that our life is not a property of ours, but it is a gift given daily and we are always amazed and grateful to be called yet again to personhood.

⚜⚜⚜⚜⚜⚜⚜

The large act of love commended in the church is hospitality, the readiness to welcome into the church and into our lives those who are alone and abandoned and needy. Hospitality is making a home for those who have been rendered homeless in our society, asking not if they are qualified but if they belong in the sphere of God's love. Given the new commandment, the gospel truth is that we cannot love God whom we have not seen, unless we love our brothers and our sisters who are right there in front of us.

⚜⚜⚜⚜⚜⚜

The quarrels we undertake are not only sometimes vicious; they are also convenient because the quarrels distract us from the main claims of the text, and so debilitate the force of the text. Of course it matters what the church decides about sexuality, but in the long run that skirmish or a dozen like it are as nothing before the truth that the therapeutic technological military consumerism cannot deliver or keep its promises. All of us—conservatives who are attentive to what the Bible says about sexuality and indifferent about the Bible on economics, and liberals who mumble about what the Bible says on sex but major in economics—all of us stand under the awareness that the primary commitments of our society amount to a choice of a path of death. The quarrels we undertake must be kept in perspective, because none of those quarrels occupy this Holy Character unduly. What counts is that we were not there at the outset of creation, and we will not be there at the curfew; our life between the outset and the curfew is the gift of the One who calls us not to assault neighbor but to be on our way in wonder, love, and praise.

⚜⚜⚜⚜⚜⚜

All of us, to some extent, hold the line against "the other." All of us, to some extent, know that our faith calls us out beyond that. Some of us are more able and more willing to enter the risk of inclusiveness, to embrace the others who threaten us. It is clear that the good news of God's love and God's healing and God's justice cannot be kept just for us and people like us. The pull of God's largeness summons all of us, often through the words and presence of "the other." The old teachings of exclusion cannot fully protect us from God's pull to be a neighbor.

❊❊❊❊❊❊❊❊

Not many of us need advice about what to do with our life. Not many of us want such advice either. We may not agree on what to do, but most of us know what we would do, if we had the wits, or the freedom, or the imagination, or the courage. The church has been longer on advice than it has been on "underneath nurture." Perhaps that is because advice is easier to give than is freedom or courage, and more obvious, too. Or perhaps it is because as liberals or as conservatives, we feel so passionately that we want to get everybody else straightened out. The problem is that the others are not very much open to coercion either, as we are not open.

It is a time, in my judgment, when the church may lower its voice about advice, and speak more gently and healthily and honestly about the nurture of faithful imagination, freedom, and courage. That stuff is not in large supply among us, and when it is not, our lives are diminished. That stuff is in short supply because such matters drive us to mystery which we cannot explain, to loyalty we cannot control, and to trust that we cannot will. Out of that mystery and loyalty and trust which comes to us as a gift, there does emerge an obedient life. But we arrive there by a route other than our zeal and certitude, and that makes us uneasy.

❧❧❧❧❧❧❧❧❧

When Paul spoke about living in harmony with one another as a gift of Christ's new regime, he knew about conflict and quarreling in his churches and all around the empire. And so do we. We imagine now that liberals and conservatives must be in conflict, and Christians and Muslims must be in shared violence with each other, and poor blacks and rich whites must compete with an edge of hate. Well, here is the news. There is a world reconciled between Jew and Greek, between male and female, between free and slave, and all the other alienations that we can name. Because Christ has broken down the walls of separation. In him all sorts of people recover their sanity and their humanity enough to see brother and sister.

❧❧❧❧❧❧❧❧❧

There is a meanness in the church, people lined up conservative and liberal, starchy and sloppy, and what happens is that the energy for mission gets transposed into having our way. But the word of life is not a liberal word or a conservative word, not a white word or a black word. It is the word beyond all our words, the word come flesh in Jesus.

❧❧❧❧❧❧❧❧❧

The poet in Isaiah 56 urges that the community of faith not act out of its fear, but out of its most treasured conviction about the large mercy and goodness of the God of Mount Sinai. The poet urges a wide-open heart to include all those who share the practices of faith in covenant.

This issue of inclusion and exclusion is endlessly a tough one. It has been tough since the time of Moses, because there really are starchy conditions of faith that cannot be compromised. Not just anybody can belong. Those conditions, however, are not external marks, but concern, intention, practice, neighbor care, Sabbath, and covenant. The conditions concern the resolve to live a different way in the world.

❧❧❧❧❧❧❧❧

So here is your mission, if you choose to accept it:

> Stand with Jews who also wait for Messiah.
> Stand with Christians who see God's power in Jesus.
> Stand with Gentiles in mercy, all the others who are not like us.
> Stand in that company and you will find yourself filled with hope for what God will yet do.

❧❧❧❧❧❧❧❧

As the Christ child comes, members of the new world imagine that we do not need to divide the world into rich and poor, black and white, Muslim and Christian and Jew, straight and gay, entitled and unentitled. Imagine that! There are those in our society who have a great stake in keeping it all adversarial. But what happens to the children of truth and hope is that such conflicts lose their power over us and their interest for us, as our fear of each other is dissipated in a common life of welcome.

❧❧❧❧❧❧❧❧

As Paul envisioned welcome of one another, he knew about a world of exclusion that is grounded in fear and anxiety. And so do we. All around now are barriers and

gates and fences that draw lines around gifts and possibilities and resources and access. The lines are drawn
closer and closer until all are excluded except the blessed,
cunning ones, and even they are left nervous about when
the next wall will be built and who will then be excluded.
Well, here is the news. Out beyond the world of exclusion and rejection and hostility, there is on offer a world
of welcome that sees the other not as threat or competitor, but as cohort on the pilgrimage of humanity. That
alternative world of welcome is signed by bread and by
wine; but it is known by lives that reach out and touch, in
order to heal and transform.

❖❖❖❖❖❖❖❖❖

I speak to you an evangelical word about belonging,
about belonging more than you know, perhaps more
than you want, belonging on which you did not vote,
belonging perhaps by baptism, and if not by baptism,
then by the wonder and surprise of your birth. Because
you were born, you belong. The assurance of belonging
is not found in some social theory, but in the strange
truth about Jesus who has broken down the walls which
divide, walls which bring fear and arrogance and hunger
and death.

❖❖❖❖❖❖❖❖❖

We live in a society that wants to sort out and divide
and alienate. Creating hostility is a big industry among
us. We live on our individualism, made of pride and
despair, that wants us not to belong. Well, the news
is we belong. You belong. We belong to each other,
because compassion has been shown to us. We are no
longer free in our pride to abuse like David. We are no
longer fated in our despair like the crowd to be endlessly

at risk. We belong to each other. We can trust in that. We can care because of that.

❧❧❧❧❧❧❧❧❧

Wherever God's demanding compassion comes, life begins anew. There is a belonging between the powerful and powerless, between great nations and exposed tribes, between Jew and Gentile, between male and female, between bright ones and struggling ones. There is a membership that cannot be disregarded. That membership requires us to end our indifference, our competition, our arrogance, our despair. Now there is a hope in the world, an insistence that together we will become a "dwelling place for God." The membership based on God's powerful compassion, on that you can count. As a result, all the outsiders have come home and are insiders, in this new humanity that is only now becoming visible.

Chapter Nine

Newness and Hope

Despair yields a culture of death ... and violence ... and brutality that is mostly unnoticed by the shoppers, attended only by an occasional poet who is either misunderstood or dismissed as a celebrity. The faithful are called before the authorities to give an alternative account of reality, an alternative consisting in imaginative leaps beyond the given, imaginative leaps that at best are gifts of God's own spirit. The question that concerns Jews and Christians is "Can we hope?"

❖❖❖❖❖❖❖❖❖

My judgment is that when hope is divided among our communities of interpretation, it is likely that our hope is lodged with an idol who cannot keep promises; it follows that hope in the promises of the true God can only be practiced as we hope together, and that in spite of all our differentiations.

❖❖❖❖❖❖❖❖❖

Hope requires a Source and Agent of newness who is, in inscrutable ways, generative, who is not imprisoned in old habits or present-tense commitments. That, of course, is a theological statement about the character of God that Jews and Christians commonly confess. Thus, I begin with the affirmation that hope is theologically grounded, which of course stacks the cards at the outset. But the alternative to such an agency that stands outside present arrangements is to find ground for hope within present life arrangements themselves, a strategy that inescapably produces the absolutizing of some power arrangement that soon or late becomes idolatrous and self-destructive.

⚜⚜⚜⚜⚜⚜⚜⚜

The new song never describes the world the way it now is. The new song imagines how the world will be in God's good time to come. The new song is a protest against the way the world now is. The new song is refusal to accept the present world as it is, a refusal to believe this is right or that the present will last. The church is always at its most daring and risking and dangerous and free when it sings a new song. Because then it sings that the power of the gospel will not let the world finally stay as it is.

⚜⚜⚜⚜⚜⚜⚜⚜

Hope requires a community of faith and action that is open to newness that will be given as a gift. Hope is indeed a communal activity, for none can fully hope alone. The intention of Holy Agency is to form communities of obedient action that rely upon and respond to divine intention. The formation and maintenance of such a community is always problematic because the many narratives of despair are, on the face of it, more impressive and more reassuring than the narratives of hope. The community of faith and action formed around Moses struggled for fidelity and sought immediately to return to Egypt for guaranteed food (Exod. 16:3); and when cut free from Egypt, that community promptly made for itself images that would witness against the free generativity of Yahweh (Exod. 32:4). It is not different, moreover, in Jesus' formation of a community of disciples who are characteristically fearful, obtuse, and unresponsive. The community of faithful obedience is thus always in jeopardy; in its jeopardy, however, it manages over time to make enough of a response to divine generativity to make its way in the world.

❊❊❊❊❊❊❊❊❊

To "the land of the living" is where God has summoned us. It lies beyond our helplessness and our hopelessness. Getting there requires honesty about our deep, failed deaths. Beyond that honesty is all the power of God, given to the ones who will receive in their need.

❊❊❊❊❊❊❊❊❊

The church and its pastors await the gift of newness from the Spirit. One of the ways in which the church and its pastors do that is that they consistently give voice and visibility to our common ambivalence whereby we are in a place for re-choosing, for re-choosing beyond all of our old, jaded options. The spirit is wind and not wall. It is possibility and not coercion. It is opportunity and not threat. And when we do wall and coercion and threat, we only imitate and replicate the dominant narrative of consumer militarism. Ours, however, is an alternative not only in outcome but also in mode. The wind, so the script says, is about

> new creation
> new freedom from slavery
> being born again

All of that is less likely behind the barricades of certitude that require us to deny so much about ourselves.
Ministry is for truth-telling about the shape we are in, all
of us together. And that truth-telling makes us free.

⚜⚜⚜⚜⚜⚜

I have deliberately used the term "imagination" because
I want to insist that such stylized narrative account is
indeed a human construction. The poets put the words
together in this particular way. The poets utilized this
pattern of worship in order to reiterate and reenact this
advocacy. It happens over and over; every time a pastor
and a choir director get together to pick hymns, the work
is one of constructive imagination designed to lead the
congregation in turn to imagine the world in a certain
way. Much worship is informed by tradition and conventional practice, but those who construct such worship
must each time commit an act of imagination in order to
determine what is to be accented and to adapt the advocacy to the specificity of context.

⚜⚜⚜⚜⚜⚜

We are the ones with attentiveness who notice here and
there God's hidden way of transformation of the world.
We watch and notice a leper cleansed, a dead person
dancing, crowds fed, justice given, bodies reclaimed. The
Easter miracles happen here and there, and the people
of God sign on for the mystery of God's transformative
work. We covet those moments when the power of death

and injustice do not prevail in the world. We bear witness to God's steadfast love.

❀❀❀❀❀❀❀

It may be a temptation to want to be transformed into the dominant images of our society and imagine it is the gospel—more winsome, more clever, more competent, more ambitious, more secure. You can hustle around and achieve, because we here are all high achievers. But that transformation finally will not do, because it is in truth not what our life is about. The transformation that counts is to embrace our oddity as creatures of God.

It may be that the temptation regarding transformation is to imagine that I am all alone and if there is to be transformation, I will have to work at it, so ten ways to a healthy body, six steps to good sex, and four disciplines for prosperity. Against all such self-help, we are being transformed, even in spite of ourselves, because God will not quit on us.

Or the temptations may be despair, knowing that in our deepest places, we resist change, do not want to change, will never be changed. But the news is that we are being changed by the power of God, won over to the purpose of God by a power that is not resisted, even by our deep despair.

❀❀❀❀❀❀❀

We are called to put on the notion that change may be more healthy than stability and constancy. Of course we all know that about many dimensions of life, but we are very slow to see in change the action of God. We have been taught that he is a God who does not change, but always provides the enduring quality in a world which seems so ephemeral. But we are discovering again in Scripture that we are caught with a God on the move, who shows himself most often not in the complacency of things as they are but in the threat of the new. And we shall have to learn to feel freshly about ourselves.

❖❖❖❖❖❖❖❖

There is an Easter revolution coming here whereby the world will be brought to new life. And we are players in that movement. It begins in vivid hope and it ends in wondrous well-being. We get from crying out to well-being by the fidelity of God. At the center of the story are bread and wine, gift, and newness. . . . It is about the God who is more ready to give gifts than we are to receive them. We stand among those who have sought and asked—and received!

❖❖❖❖❖❖❖❖

As you tell the truth that breaks denial, so become a "hope-teller" that breaks the spell of despair. Do you imagine, as do many, that there is no way out of our moral morass, our ideological fantasies, our burden of a world mismanaged and irreversible? Do you imagine a church so preoccupied with ideological passion that it has no energy for mission and leaves you weary and without hope? Well, take a Sabbath rest and become a hope-teller, a poet of "assurance of things hoped for, the conviction of things not seen." Take a Sabbath from despair by the staggering truth that Christ is risen and that creation surges with the Easter power of new life that God is now giving. Tell hope that knows that the brick quotas of fear and coercion and usurpation are about to end. Tell hope that does not depend on our conservative certitude or on our liberal self-assuredness, but only on the God who has given the Easter verdict over a new world and called it "very good."

⚜⚜⚜⚜⚜⚜⚜⚜

What has become new, by the mercy of God, is that the recruitment of Jesus of Nazareth as the harbinger of a new world has now in turn gathered a new community of the faithful who become the ground of God's good laughter in the contemporary world. It is the body of Christ in the world, gathered from all nations, that is now recruited to perform God's governance in the world. That rule, we now know in light of Friday, is a rule of vulnerability that heals and reconciles and transforms and forgives. It is a rule that contradicts the aggression of the nations that keep imagining that raw power coupled with ruthless technology is the wave of the future. That rule, we now know in light of Sunday, is a rule of joy that surprises and elates and generates new possibilities.

⚜⚜⚜⚜⚜⚜⚜⚜

Hope requires a text that mediates between holy generativity and communal obedience. This mediating text that is a primal connection between holy generativity and communal obedience is perforce an odd text, or in the words of Karl Barth, always "strange and new." Over time, there are many strategies to try to make manageable what is strange and to make commonplace what is new; such strategies, however, cannot in the long run succeed, because of the character of the text itself and because of the Character who occupies the text. That is why, on the one hand, there are endless quarrels about the text and why, on the other hand, the interpretive protagonists agree in a rough way that the text is revelatory, offering glimpses of that which remains hidden from us.

As the text mediates between holy generativity and communal obedience, hope requires communities of interpretation that are emancipated, emancipatory, generative, and daring in their interpretation. These communities at the same time, however, have found ways to resist the generative force of interpretation, whether by fundamentalist reductionism or by critical explanation, for both reductionism and explanation inescapably curb the dangerous subversive force of a text that witnesses to hidden holy mystery.

⚜⚜⚜⚜⚜⚜

We have prayed that God's will may be done on earth as it is in heaven (Matt. 6:10). We have imagined how it is in heaven and have petitioned that earth should be the same. Even in our praying, however, we did not know the earth could be transformed. We believed that our cities are hopeless, that our policies and practices must be endlessly filled with poison and death. All of that destructiveness, however, has run out of steam and authority. A Newness is coming beyond our power to speak or to start. It is a newness rooted in God's own power, now coming to embodiment in human, earthly, public form.

⚜⚜⚜⚜⚜⚜

God, the one with grace and mercy, is a God of justice, righteousness, and truth. The world is not up for grabs. It is not available for our silliness or for our violence or for our pollution or for our wealth or for our fear or for our power. We have seen traces of God. We have seen traces in Jesus of Nazareth. We have seen there enough about mercy and grace and justice and truth. We have seen enough of this God to make the journey beyond our many failures. God goes with us into the newness, and we are on our way, rejoicing in the power of the Spirit.

❦❦❦❦❦❦❦❦❦

Pentecost is not just about a babble in the midst of confusion. Pentecost is about a liberated future that God has promised and that God will give. The same God who causes strangeness in the past is the God who gives newness in the future.

❦❦❦❦❦❦❦❦❦

What a stunning vocation for the church, to stand free and hope-filled in a world gone fearful, and to think, imagine, dream, vision a future that God will yet enact. What a work of visioning for the church when society all around is paralyzed in fear, preoccupied by commodity, mesmerized by wealth, seeking endless power, and deeply, deeply frightened. And here is this little community of visited people, not greedy, not fearful, not in despair . . . dreaming about the way of peace among peoples . . . visioning about justice between haves and have-nots . . . prophesying about an ordered earth, of greed curbed enough to respect the needs of the environment . . . not defensive about the others, but able to be inclusive of those not like us.

This community has no doubt that God's good world to come is not in the past, it is not in heaven, but it is on the earth, beyond bloody fear and scary chaos. What a place for the church to be on Pentecost!

❦❦❦❦❦❦❦❦❦

The news is that God wills that strange chaos of exile. God wills the dismantling of our world, for that is where promise has a chance. But the more decisive news is that we will laugh later, the laugh of Sarah, the Easter laugh of Jesus, the cosmic laugh of God whose kingdom will have no end. We shall, along with our tired world, be remade for singing and praising and yielding, and communing and obeying. We shall be remade along with our world which is now too prudent, too cunning, too coercive. We shall be remade according to God's powerful hope. We can in our fear and complacency resist the cry and so preclude the laugh, and hope for business as usual, world without end. But in that way lies only killing and dying. It is "this other way" that leads us to say with our community: "Beloved, we are God's children now; it does not yet appear what we shall be, but we know that when he appears we shall be like him, for we shall see him as he is" (1 John 3:2). We shall be like him: like him feasting, like him with fear finished, like him with bread abounding, like him learning war no more . . . like him, but it begins in the way of the loss we cry for the whole failed creation. It begins there. It ends in utter joy. It ends in a laugh that echoes the gracious, majestic laugh of God.

⚜⚜⚜⚜⚜⚜⚜

Hope in gospel faith is not just a vague feeling that things will work out, for it is evident that things will not just work out. Rather, hope is the conviction, against a great deal of data, that God is tenacious and persistent in overcoming the deathliness of the world, that God intends joy and peace. Christians find compelling evidence, in the story of Jesus, that Jesus, with great persistence and great vulnerability, everywhere he went, turned the enmity of society toward a new possibility, turned the sadness of the world toward joy, introduced a new regime where the dead are raised, the lost are found, and the displaced are brought home again. We draw our hope from the breath-taking memory of this Jesus!

⚜⚜⚜⚜⚜⚜⚜

Hope is the deep religious conviction that God has not quit.

⚜⚜⚜⚜⚜⚜⚜

"He will baptize you with the Holy Spirit" (Luke 3:16). I imagine that sounds as weird to you as it does to me. And I imagine it sounded odd to them. We who are relatively affluent and relatively sophisticated do not talk that way, do not expect it, and do not welcome it. In truth, however, being baptized with God's holy spirit does not mean goofy charismatic acting out. It means, I take it, we may be visited by a spirit of openness, generosity, energy, that "the force" may come over us, carry us to do obedient things we have not yet done, kingdom things we did not think we had in us, neighbor things from which we cringe, because newness is on its way among us.

⚜⚜⚜⚜⚜⚜⚜

Hezekiah began to accommodate political-economic realities, and the hope of liturgy largely disappeared. But Israel, not the last to do so, preferred the liturgy to reality so they kept singing and they kept hoping:

> They sang and hoped for someone who would be filled with God's spirit;
> They sang and hoped for the good judge of the poor to come;
> They sang and hoped for a restored rehabilitated creation.

They hoped and they sang. And every time they sang, they refused the fearful reality all around them. Every time they hoped, they gathered their energy for new faith and courage in the world.

⚜⚜⚜⚜⚜⚜⚜⚜⚜

The poet in Isaiah 40 will not succumb or concede to the fearful, but also fearing, tenuous power of the empire, because the world could not be sponsored or sustained by such a deathly power. The creation belongs (and so do you) not to the life-denying, world-destroying, faith-nullifying empire, but to the God who cares in seeming absence and who governs in seeming defeat. The resigned ones are called to enter the poem, to touch the source of life behind and beyond the empire, to embrace the real situation which is in the company of God whom the empire cannot dethrone. Have you not known, have you not heard? That the world belongs to this God who is a self-starter, and who holds the world and us in a massive will for life.

⚜⚜⚜⚜⚜⚜⚜⚜⚜

The good news is that we need not serve the wrong god, trust the wrong life-giver, fear the wrong power. We may read life differently, and the way to do that is to wait in eager longing, for the God of creation and rescue to work a new way in the world, to wait in keen expectation, to wait in active zeal, receiving every hint of newness and acting on it, to be ready to go for the gift of life, to leave off fear, intimidation, resignation, pooped out-ness, as the governance works a newness.

⚜⚜⚜⚜⚜⚜⚜⚜⚜

What Paul knows and what the church has always known is that the power of death is on the loose in the world, all those forces—personal, social, and cosmic— that want to negate our lives and reduce them to empty dread, gnawing at us, eroding us, talking us out of our true selves. And then comes the Easter force, the power of God to bring newness. Paul is not hung up on curious questions of what happened on that odd Sunday. For the church always knows the present tense, not just a Sunday morning long ago, but the present tense that God's powerful force for life has been unleashed in the world.

⁜⁜⁜⁜⁜⁜⁜⁜⁜

Imagine, as Jesus imagines, a company of disciples who have not snuggled into the present, but now are Easter hopers. Because Easter hopers are able to be odd, able to have courage, able to receive newness from God that the world does not expect. To them Jesus says, "Leap for joy!" Newness comes!

⁜⁜⁜⁜⁜⁜⁜⁜⁜

The gospel is a welcome to the land of the living for those who have relied upon God in their most elemental exhaustion. Consider who is in the land of the living. Not all the pretenders who imagine they are buoyant and beautiful. Not all the grim people who want to scold and control. Not all the people who think and act exactly like us. No, the land of the living is for those who in fact are recovering . . . recovering from alcohol, from anger and greed and lust and despair and selfishness and sexism and racism and ageism, people who have put their fear and anger and rage all behind them, because they have turned their failed lives over to God. They have been addressed by God's word urging them to "come out." They have been blown on by God's wind, so that the bones rattle to newness.

❁❁❁❁❁❁❁❁❁

Resurrection of the dead is God's capacity to take a circumstance of complete shutdown and hopelessness and make something new from it. Easter is the parade example of God's readiness for newness that the world knows as inexplicable miracle. All around that parade example, however, are gifts and surprises that permit us to breathe and to dance and to live in ways we did not expect. It is all resurrection!

❁❁❁❁❁❁❁❁❁

God is a self-starter who starts the world again when we can see no newness on the horizon. The good news is surely an urgent word of assurance in our time, because our society and our world are close to shutdown and no one can see ahead. But women and men of faith know otherwise. We do not know because of great policies or big strategies. We do not know because of great resources or secret information. We know because we are part of the story of an alternative of new possibility, grounded in unconditional love, right in the middle of our lives. And we can see it welling up in specific ways when people give themselves over to the goodness of God.

❁❁❁❁❁❁❁❁❁

Imagine that among us: The God of new creation and assured life wills newness. Those who trust soar. Those who believe move on. Those who know can dance and sing and risk and care. We are all children of Abraham and Sarah, a new heir, a fresh start, a new possibility, even a new city. We do not serve the gods of the old systems, but the God of faithful freedom who gives life to the dead and who calls into existence the things that do not exist.

❖❖❖❖❖❖❖❖❖

People like us are not into abrupt change or heroic action. We walk up to God's newness only carefully, only suspiciously, only selectively. The beginning point for us may be, because the great public questions may be too demanding and too scary, to reflect on the fresh summons to the self. Our selves are mostly situated in old, defining memories that we received in older, better days. The gospel is always a call out from such old certainties to God's newness. Who knows if we could risk turning loose. We might be as surprised as jackals and ostriches when we find fresh water, fresh spirit, fresh life. We might join the beasts of the wilderness with new songs of praise, doxology, and amazement. A life sounded in new praise is one no longer held in old memory, old guilt, old fear, or old weariness. It is all a staggering newness now offered, out beyond our many exiles, toward home. Do you not perceive it?

❖❖❖❖❖❖❖❖❖

The singers generated songs. The songs became text. And the text was to be read and reread, heard and reheard, interpreted and reinterpreted. It is a community of equilibrium that can confine texts to one meaning. By contrast a community of hope has texts that always "mean" afresh; hopers engaged inescapably in the juggling act of interpretation that defiantly moves between acquiescence to present arrangements and risk that opens through many layers of imagination and polyvalence. Such layered interpretation refuses closure, for the closure of the text would only bespeak the closure of the empire and, before that, the closure of the brickyard.

⚜⚜⚜⚜⚜

The sentinel noticed the movement of the troops and drew the conclusion: "Fallen, fallen is Babylon!" The truth of our evangelical moment is that Babylon has fallen and is always falling. The power of the empire, the regime of old truth, cannot withstand the new power of life that comes among us. What a burden! What a risk! What a marvel to be present and uttering as the new truth delegitimates and deconstructs what is old and failed. The newness comes in with and under utterance. And we are the ones!

⚜⚜⚜⚜⚜

God's miracles are like this: new life and new gift well up in ways we do not understand. There is slippage in our management of the world. There is mystery that subverts our best calculations, and life seeps through the cracks with newness that we cannot make for ourselves.

⚜⚜⚜⚜⚜

To "be glorified with Christ" is to be present with Jesus in the astonishing Easter wonder when new life erupts in the midst of death, when new love overwhelms old hates, when new justice breaks the grip of old injustice, when perfect love casts out fear and resentment. We are as new as resurrection day.

⚜⚜⚜⚜⚜

Our Easter participation is not dramatic. It is to think and to act toward newness when we awaken to the awareness that the world belongs to God and not to us, that the range of God's compassion for the world is to us and through us and beyond us.

❧❧❧❧❧❧❧❧❧❧

The poet invites his people to turn from the defeated idols of old-age denial to the powerful news of life, given by the righteous savior who fashions a new world. The new world will not be old, tired Jerusalem revisited. The new world will not be a recurrence of old symptoms, old vicious cycles, old games people play, but a new mode of life marked by compassion, hospitality, justice, wholeness. And God will work it.

❧❧❧❧❧❧❧❧❧❧

Is it true that when we look, the earth is formless and void and the hills quiver and the world is emptied of people and beasts? Is it true that God said chaos is not the place of my action, but the power for life overrides to form a newness? Is it true that we will laugh as we watch the new world form? Is it true that letting go permits newness? Is it true that alluding to cosmic hurt permits personal possibility? Is it true that releasing old idols offers a way for the God of life who is beyond our control yet within our gift? Yes, yes, yes! The church says yes. The new Jerusalem shouts affirmation. The cloud of witnesses verifies the poets. Life is not a syllogism of theology, or a blueprint of morality, or a scheme of therapy, but an odd tale told by people who have stories of concrete transformation, of facing chaos and receiving new life, of laughing deeply at God's joy, and God's gift, and God's victory, and daring to mock the chaos that has lost its power.

❧❧❧❧❧❧❧❧❧❧

We must forget and we must remember. I suspect sometimes the church tends to remember just what it should
forget, and to forget just what it should remember.
Remembering and forgetting is a delicate matter. And it
may be best summarized in the song we have sung. We do
love to tell the old, old story. That is our best remembering. But we live in the hope (and this is forgetting) that
the old, old story should become the new, new song. We
do not know how that should happen. But it is promised
to those who risk the memory for the sake of the hope.

Chapter Ten

Public Witness and Responsibility

Now is the time for our expectations of the church to grow. We must expect of the church

- that it continue to tell the truth about the great issues of the day,
- that it continue the wonderful gossip about the little network that we are, and
- that it continue to pull us toward strange voices that are beyond our own.

❦❦❦❦❦❦❦❦❦

There is a lot of religious craziness going around. It has to do with "follow your bliss." Or more popularly, "I am not religious, but I am spiritual." The import of such a mantra, now often repeated, is that it can just be "me"; that is all I need for the religious dimension of my life, rather like the "free market system" in religion. Well, you can indeed have religion that way; but you cannot have the God of the gospel all alone. What we need for the truth of the gospel is a community that has staying power, a tradition that has depth, and a missional mandate that pulls us beyond ourselves. Because gospel truth is not a private deal in which we are not inconvenienced.

❖❖❖❖❖❖❖❖❖

There are very few folk left to tell truth among us and even fewer to tell hope among us. So I bid you imagine that your parish is one of those rare places in your town or city where the truth can be told,

> about militarism,
> about consumerism,
> about anti-neighborliness,
> about violence.

And your parish is one of the few venues where hope can be told:

> A love that will not let us go,
> because our hope is in no other save in thee alone.

❖❖❖❖❖❖❖❖❖

The chaos we now face in our world is huge and deep and costly and fearful. But the Jesus people have work to do . . . work in the neighborhood, work at public policy, work that begins at the Holy Table. The work is to look the chaos in the face and then to make a commitment to God's new creation.

❖❖❖❖❖❖❖❖❖

God has called us to immense responsibility, not to use the earth, but to care for the earth. In a society where we are all shoppers and users and consumers, the gospel calls every human person to be a manager of life's resources in ways that enhance the common good. We meet regularly to ask together, "What needs to be done to help the earth function more fully?" to let the community be more human, to let our society be a place of well-being for all?

⚜⚜⚜⚜⚜⚜⚜

The issues that make for conflict in the church today are not issues created by some angry people, but they are issues that touch deeply the very core of our faith. We can eliminate the voices that threaten, we can silence the sounds we don't like, we can change the scene, we can transfer the action. What we cannot do is avoid the call to maturity that is in the gospel. And that call is to put off what we cherish and put on what we fear and loathe.

⚜⚜⚜⚜⚜⚜⚜

We are called to put on love for the world, the world we have been taught deep in our bones to fear and hate and resist. But we did not learn so from Christ, rather we learned God so loved the world. So in our maturing we need to ask how we feel about the world of arms and poverty and TV and mobility and pressure and pace and people and problems. This is so very new for many of us, and the church stands accused of not helping us love this world where God has placed us.

We shall have to put on the notion that life, in all its abundance, comes from involvement. But our monastic ideals, which have been transformed only slightly into our suburban detachment, have taught us to avoid and keep clear and stay detached. But we did not learn so from Jesus. We learned about the involved life from manger to cross with the road between littered with need and filth and joy and all the humanness of the world into which he came. The life of Jesus speaks so eloquently about the joy and pain of involvement, and it calls us to unlearn our non-Christian notion of detachment from the hurt of the world.

❖❖❖❖❖❖❖❖❖

The Bible is not excessively religious. It has no abiding interest in heaven, except it knows that a new heaven always yields a new earth. We religious people dare not prattle about God in heaven if we do not do the hard work of the new earthly derivation.

❖❖❖❖❖❖❖❖❖

We are only concerned about witnesses and testimony when truth and its claims are contested and it becomes necessary to go to court. When there is enough agreement on the truth of the matter to settle out of court, no witnesses need to be called, no depositions need to be taken, and no testimony need be offered.

There was a long time when the claims of the Christian faith were so easily accommodated in US culture that there were no disputes about the truth. The church mostly did not think about the dangerous task of testimony . . . martyr . . . that is the Greek word for witnesses. The notion of testimony as a risky enterprise seemed like an ancient, old-fashioned idea that no longer pertained in a modern, gentle society of consensus.

Of late, however, truth is again contested even among us. The need for adjudication of the truth arises in part as a product of bewilderment as we live in a newly strange world. It arises in part as well as a consequence of deeply felt, strongly invested advocacies that butt against each other and that cannot be readily reconciled. In such an environment, dispute is inescapable and therefore the need for witnesses.

❧❧❧❧❧❧❧❧❧

The substance of Christian faith, the body of conviction and teaching, is not a private deal, not only an immediate experience we may embrace, but it is a long, slow conversation kept alive for us by lots of hard work over many generations. That faith has been kept alive by mothers and fathers who are terribly ordinary people. It has also been kept alive by powerful and bold witnesses who have invested their lives in dangerous ways, because they had a different fix on reality.

❧❧❧❧❧❧❧❧❧

We are called to see that the meaning of the Christian life is in the construction of just and equitable social structures and institutions. And of course that means giving up much of the paternalism of a love-ethic that encouraged generosity but not the reconstruction of the social order. That is a very difficult thing for many persons to face up to, because we have been in league with a God who is kind and generous and rather naive. But we did not learn so from Christ. In him we see a God who creates and destroys kingdoms, who challenges governments and social systems, who intervenes for humanity against the most developed and sophisticated forms of inhumanity. We shall have to put on the recognition that we are members of a social system called to responsibility for what that system does to persons.

❧❧❧❧❧❧❧❧❧

The cruciality of this ministry is not that the church may prosper. It is that the world may live (and not die) and rejoice (and not cower). The reason this ministry is so crucial is that for the most part there are none except the church in its better days—and the synagogue and the mosque on their better days—to mediate irascible holiness as newness, to evoke consequent ambivalence, to manage that ambivalence toward newness, and then to wait. The dominant script of therapeutic technological consumer militarism does none of that:

- It does not mediate irascible holiness or acknowledge it.
- It does not evoke or acknowledge consequent ambivalence.
- It cannot manage ambivalence toward newness.
- It does not wait.

Ministry, with all the cost and joy of discipleship, is urgent among us, as urgent as it is wondrous and difficult and amazing and disconcerting. It is indeed a treasure in earthen vessels.

❦❦❦❦❦❦❦❦

The world is waiting for Christians who are not angry or anxious or weary or quarrelsome or cynical or in despair. The world is waiting for folk who trust enough to move out beyond themselves.

❦❦❦❦❦❦❦❦

The church exists so that the city can have its own true self. Jesus—and the church—can show the city through its life and our ministry the things that make for peace. Jesus—and the church—can show the city by his life and our ministry, the things that make for mercy and justice and compassion and reconciliation, the things that make a city a viable human community.

The church, after Jesus, has this Friday truth to tell the city, that suffering love is the only viable form of public life. The church, after Jesus, has this Sunday truth to tell the city, that God's gift of new life permits quite different patterns of money and power, of housing and health and jobs and water and justice, all new possibilities because in Easter the world has begun again under new governance.

✤✤✤✤✤✤✤✤

The church in this truth-telling vocation is not preoccupied with itself, even with its survival. It is clear that the church is not to be an escape from the reality of the city. It is rather summoned by the gospel to be a major player in the city, that even the city may reflect on the rule of the God of Israel who is also our Lord and Savior. Jesus has wept over the city, but is ready, soon enough, to laugh an Easter laugh over the city, filled with joy and hope when the city becomes a genuine neighborhood. We may be the ones who can turn the weeping of Jesus to the joy of an urban Easter of new life. It requires that we think and live ourselves differently in the place where God has put us.

✤✤✤✤✤✤✤✤

The church loves to quarrel about social policy and justice and taxes and entitlements. There are those who think this is not our business in the church. But they are wrong, because we have been baptized. And being baptized means we are no longer of those who are selfish and greedy and preoccupied with ourselves, for we have been baptized into a new story of Jesus and our life is marked by generosity, grace, and forgiveness, especially toward the disabled who we—like Jesus—call forward for healing.

※※※※※※

We are the ones who cry out in hope and indignation, because the world is not right. The world in its desert hunger, its fearful injustice, its destabilizing storms of finance and sexuality, its captivity, its brutality, its inhumanity needs a voice for the cry of advocacy. And we are designated to be the ones who speak insistently to God on behalf of the world, that the world may be changed.

※※※※※※

The church is now in a struggle for the truth of the gospel; perhaps it always is. The church is seduced that it should settle for pietism in an extravagant US entitlement, so that Jesus does not disturb. The church is tempted to turn this Jesus into a contest so we all take our little piece of ideological truth and imagine it big. The church is tempted to forget the deep, thick claim of God's holiness and flatten the vision of Jesus into a social program. But the doxology keeps Jesus elusive and out beyond us, full of grace and truth, full of sovereignty and power, full of Friday death and full of Sunday life . . . and we are called to obedience.

※※※※※※

We must understand our faith in large, public categories, because God's purposes are not worked out in our small zones of piety, but in the great affairs of state where folk are either crushed or valued.

※※※※※※

In the United States, evangelism is a very confused business, all tied up with strategies, church growth, and new members. Evangelism, however, is much simpler than that. It means simply to bring more and more of our life under the rule of this one loyalty and purpose and will, it means to trust the news, the announcement of a new governance, and then to act accordingly, gladly to turn zones of our life over to this purpose, and to hold nothing back.

❧❧❧❧❧❧❧❧❧

This is a most dangerous and exotic time for the community of Jesus in America. It is a dangerous time in Western culture for any who care about humanness and humaneness. This is no time for business as usual. Because the old modes of so much science have failed. Our old slogans for organizing power have now exhausted them. We are at the brink of something new in our society that could be marvelously healing or dangerously destructive. I submit that around the edges of our culture, the healing power of Jesus is at the edge of new possibility. You in this generation now have new questions before you that lie at the edge of our awareness. But they are urgent. They have to do with whether the healing of the nations and the healing of human community and the healing of human persons is possible in this world so bent toward death.

❧❧❧❧❧❧❧❧❧

The news is that this is not a world without God. For that reason, there are limits to chaos and threat. Our society talks and acts as though it was chaos all the way down. But faith knows better. God is God. Baptized people are baptized to respond to threat with confidence in God's goodness, to answer anxiety with freedom, to have a kind of buoyancy for the neighborhood that the world does not understand. Our society wants us to live always on alert. But baptism says "No," because God is on the alert.

❧❧❧❧❧❧❧❧❧

In a church that cares about the quality of human life and the practice of civic well-being, the power of self-ishness and greed, of violence and brutality and indifference seems very close to the jugular of our community. One notes the convergence of the personal incidence of brutality, the unresponsiveness of public policy concerning human hurt, the shameless exploitation of public trust for greedy gain; this is the stuff of wickedness. One can despair enough to ask, will evil prevail? Is that what God wants? Have I had it wrong? The answers of the Psalmist are with a terrible tenacity: No, the stuff of injustice and exploitation are not God's will. No, that way will not prevail. No, God has not caved in. No, the world is not morally indifferent. No, no, no!

❧❧❧❧❧❧❧❧❧

The urgent news is that our society is on the way to our common death, by greed, by lust, by indifference, by cynicism, by despair, by a thousand forms of violence and brutality. That is the main story. And in the midst of all that, Jesus has put this little community that may make a difference. Reverse the process. Break the cycles. Practice our God-given humanness and gather the power and love and the self-discipline to do it.

❧❧❧❧❧❧❧❧❧

God's speech is an invitation to us to participate in the healing of the world, living to create blessing. That task is done in many ways and by many means. Conservatives want to bless the neighbor through the private sector. Liberals want to bless the neighbor by government policy. Generous people want to bless by concrete neighborly acts. The vision is of all kinds of people in all kinds of ways, many strategies, many daring acts of imagination, many gestures of kindness and generosity, many commitments to justice and peace in the world, all making a difference in the world. To cause blessing is to transmit God's power for life that God gives us to others, because we are channels for that power and not reservoirs, the force of blessing given that flows through our lives and out beyond us to others. All the others!

Chapter Eleven

Relinquishment

The word we will be given in gospel freedom is not a nice word about a nice world. It is rather a true word about our bodies and our body politic, the bodies infused with God's truth, but nonetheless temporary, passing, fragile, mortal.

❧❧❧❧❧❧❧❧

We have so much relinquishing to do in order to come to God's goodness. It is in relinquishing to God's goodness that we come to gospel freedom. That relinquishing takes the form of open-handedness, and honesty, and joyousness, ready to live the good news fully.

❧❧❧❧❧❧❧❧

To forgo the joys of our childishness for our adulthood always comes with a bit of agony and stress, because we are talking about the things we have gotten comfortable with, things we have learned to value and live by. Indeed, we are talking about those arrangements of our personal existence that have seemed eternally valid. The things

we have become accustomed to are the things that seem
right and good and ordained of God. And there is sticki-
ness because none of us is a free person. For all of our
wanting to be modern and emancipated, each of us finds
it difficult to put things off.

❖❖❖❖❖❖❖❖❖

Moaning and grieving and weeping have to do with relinquishment, about which we are always reluctant. I think,
to the point, that the church's struggle about welcoming
gays and lesbians is not much about sexuality. It is about
clinging to an old world we could manage wherein we
felt safe. We always fight a rearguard action against relinquishment, if not gays, then Muslims, and if not Muslims,
then immigrants, and after immigrants we will find new
candidates for whom to draw a line against relinquishment. It is a common temptation among conservatives
and among liberals, for nobody I know wants readily to
give up what we treasure.

❖❖❖❖❖❖❖❖❖

There is a mistaken noncovenantal notion about God that
is floating around. It teaches that God is all-sufficient, all
unto himself, supremely alone, detached, immovable, all
knowing, all ruling, all present, but beyond all the risks
and hurts and pains. That is a terribly uncovenantal God
and one from whom there is no good news. If we want
a God who just stands there and watches and governs,
that's it.

But let us be clear. That is not the God of the Bible.
Nor is that the God for whom we wait. Against all of that,
the God of the Bible is one who deeply commits himself
in irreversible ways to creation and to humankind, who
enters into covenant and who stays in solidarity with

sinful, hurting, suffering humanity. And there is such solidarity in this covenant God makes, that the pain of the world becomes the pain of God. And the news is that God does not back off from all of that. Now this means that the main mark of this God is not, first of all, omnipotence or omniscience or omnipresence, but it is fidelity, faithfulness, the readiness to stay with and stay for the hurting ones.

❖❖❖❖❖❖❖❖

We cannot be for the missional gospel and then use our energy trying to control things on our own terms. We must decide and always decide again for the sake of the gospel. And when we decide for the goodness and generosity of God, we become a different kind of people in the world.

❖❖❖❖❖❖❖❖

Weep now! Jesus does not mean to sit around and sob. He means rather to raise our voice for the grief of the world wherein our cynical power serves to produce widows, orphans, and refugees, to invest our bodies in the hurt of the world, to sound and act protest in hope, to sound and act solidarity in need, to sound and act so that transformative power goes out from our bodies to the ones without resources. Lament is not nice bourgeoisie therapy. It is the very grief of God over every Jerusalem that does not know the things that make for peace. It is the rumbling of God on behalf of the hungry when there is in fact enough food. It is the indignation of God on behalf of the poor when there is in fact enough to go around of housing and education and justice. It is the groan of God on behalf of the raped earth, when we would rather laugh in our devouring than to repent of our wasteful coveting. It is the slow, teasing hammering of God of plowshares and pruning hooks while the world rushes to the madness of swords and spears.

⚜⚜⚜⚜⚜⚜

God runs through alienation, into the silence of pain, and on to healing newness. That is the story of the day. That is the story of Jerusalem in Jeremiah, of defeat, displacement, and restoration. That is the story of Jesus, of Friday abandonment, Saturday depth, and Sunday readiness. It is the story that lets us read our own story afresh. There is a season of loss not to be avoided, a hope beyond, and a deep time of brooding between.

⚜⚜⚜⚜⚜⚜

The world will not be saved by people who stay as they are, where they are. It will be saved and healed and blessed and transformed by people who receive the evangelical imperative from God and respond. Thus, the question left to haunt us: what do we have to leave in order to go when God calls? Well, try these: our security patterns . . . our entitlements . . . our presuppositions that self-serve . . . our being so much at home that our faith turns to complacency, when caring turns to convenience.

⚜⚜⚜⚜⚜⚜

The land of promise is not in hand, always out front, awaited, always taken in hope. We have at present too many immediate examples of promised lands possessed, and then distorted into autonomy and arrogance and violence. Go, go further, go different, go. Does it strike you as it strikes me how odd this is, how dangerous and countercultural is the speech of God that turns the world? Because popular religion in our society is all about settling and being so situated as to be safe and secure beyond every adventure, "safe and secure from all alarms." But not with this God. Not with this faith. Not this people. Not this utterance that will turn the world. So we are left—we who have responded to the gospel—we are left with when and how and where to go, even when we are not particularly in a "following" mode.

✤✤✤✤✤✤✤✤

God's imperative that is terse and uncompromising is followed by a promise from God that is wide and deep, that we trust without qualification. It is as if God knew that being an antidote to a dysfunctional world is a big, hard, dangerous, demanding assignment. It causes one to be uprooted, off balance, at risk. And so comes this divine promise. "I will go with you . . . you not alone, but with me." God aligns God's self with those who leave their convenience and security in order to make a difference in the world. The God of the Bible is not rooted to place or to program, or to slogan, or to party or an ideology. . . . This is a "people God," traveling with, going before.

✤✤✤✤✤✤✤✤

That is how it is with the people who are serious about Jesus. Nothing spectacular, just a slow, steady resolve to live differently, to let the world live differently. First, do no harm. Second, forgive. The world wretchedly waits to be forgiven, seven times a day, any day, every day. Those who forgive are likely to be those close to Jesus, close to a holy call, close to a different vocation, an odd identity. We will not be thanked much. But a difference can be made. And that is enough.

✤✤✤✤✤✤✤✤

It is no wonder that the disciples respond to the imperative of Jesus by saying, "Increase our faith." Make us able
to do what you command us to do. The disciples are able
to recognize that this is a huge, difficult mandate, to be
forgivers. They reckon that they do not have the faith or
the courage or the guts to do what Jesus commands. To
forgive is to move in to break the vicious cycles of destructiveness that are all around us, whereby a hurt evokes a
hurt in response, until you have an arms race in Northern
Ireland or Israel or in the world, or in the church, or in
our families, because hitting back and getting even are
the order of the day, a common mean spirit. And now
Jesus says: "My folk act differently about morality, about
power, about money. Do not act like the world!"

⚜⚜⚜⚜⚜⚜⚜⚜⚜

This invitation of Jesus to cry now and laugh later is a
promise to you as well as to the others. It is an invitation
that you also should weep now, that you do the hurtful,
scary relinquishment of the world you have arranged, that
you live in, in dread or in delight, that you acknowledge
the world you gather around you is in deep jeopardy, that
you turn your heart and your eyes away from the contained private world of competence and congruence to the
deep pain of the large world ending, that you face what it
means in your very body that our criteria of certitude, our
canon of competence, our trustworthy modes of explanation are now all exposed as tentative and called to a deep
accountability. We are called to live at weighty risk toward
a new world whose shape we cannot see, but coming it is.

⚜⚜⚜⚜⚜⚜⚜⚜⚜

Every teenager thinks safety depends on being first,
being best, being funniest, being wildest . . . every

young sales rep has to push and push to establish worth
. . . every academic has to publish to succeed, or, as we
say, "perish." Invent yourself or you are lost and will
disappear from the landscape. Here is the good news
Before you do anything or accomplish anything or succeed at anything, you are known, you are named. You
need not fear that you will be forgotten or abandoned or
unnoticed, because, says the deep throat of God's own
voice: I have called you by name; you are mine; I love
you; I am with you.

⚜⚜⚜⚜⚜⚜

Fasting is not rejecting food. . . . It is not being seduced
by the gifts of this age.

⚜⚜⚜⚜⚜⚜

Maturity is so tricky, isn't it? We do not get more mature
by living longer but by making today's decisions in light
of today's situation and today's resources. Maturity is
not getting older and losing the enthusiasm of youth.
Maturity is not automatic, it is not a gift given us but
it is a task assigned to us, an invitation extended to us.
Maturity is not, in the context of Christian faith, being
well-adjusted so that one simply lets all the issues fly
by without challenge. Paul uses a curious phrase for the
word we translate into maturity; he says, the completed
man, measured by Christ. The man who has come of
age in terms of his discernment of who Jesus is. Let me
offer a definition of what this means: maturity is being
able to take off and to put on with graciousness. So Paul
writes: "You were taught to put away your former way
of life, your old self, corrupt and deluded by its lusts,
and to be renewed in the spirit of your minds, and to
clothe yourselves with the new self, created according to

the likeness of God in true righteousness and holiness."
(Eph. 4:22–23)

⚜⚜⚜⚜⚜⚜⚜

We people of faith do not have life on our terms. And we
have to decide that we will walk into the future on terms
other than our own.

⚜⚜⚜⚜⚜⚜⚜

We modern Protestants are a curious contradiction about
many things. About some things we want people to give
us answers and we would do anything rather than have to
make up our own minds; and yet at the same time we covet
a kind of freedom which protects us in case the answer book
doesn't yield the answer we want. But behind that lies the
need for certainty from somebody; if not the church, then
the university, and we are now living in a world where all
such authority is precarious at best, a fraud at worst. Not
many of us know what to do in a world where authority of
every kind is now radically questioned.

⚜⚜⚜⚜⚜⚜⚜

We are called to put away our false notions of self and the
feelings we have about our persons. This false notion so
much fostered by the monastic ideal—and now strangely
embraced by Playboy philosophy—has taught us that we
are souls or spirits and that's where the issues are faced.
This gives us a certain freedom about our body because
it doesn't count, so depending on how we feel, we can
either abuse it or enjoy it, but it is not the place of meaning. And this view of my body as detached from me has
led to a detached view about society and politics and economics and all the great issues of life. But we are called
to give this up, for the gospel is that we are not spirits

or souls, but bodies who must come to terms with each other and with ourselves.

✿✿✿✿✿✿✿✿✿

Our usual way is one of stiff self-reliance. Just go from strength to strength. That is a way in the world. It is, however, a way of alienation and isolation and finally anxiety. We gather to ask about another way, a way of truth-telling, a way of glad-yielding, a way of confident asking, a way of being summoned and called to account and given life we cannot take for ourselves.

✿✿✿✿✿✿✿✿✿

The discipleship of Jesus summons us to a life that is against our seduced, conventional way of living, because our conventional way is to avoid suffering, and to reject such matters as risk and cost, yielding and loss of self-control.

✿✿✿✿✿✿✿✿✿

We are in our day called to put off false notions of goodness and piety that have an incredible grip upon us. Each of us has learned from baby times that goodness means to stay clear of things, to keep clean and remain uninvolved. We have come to think of all of life like a stranger with candy, and all of us know you don't seek involvement there.

✿✿✿✿✿✿✿✿✿

We must think rather precisely about self-denial, for it is so easily misunderstood and exploited in our culture. Denial of self does not mean to be masochistic or self-abusive, or to pretend that we are other than we truly are. It does not mean little freakish resolves about watermelon during Lent or a sour, unhappy face that is humorless, as though God is pleased by our embrace of wretchedness. The church in the United States has a sad history of confusing discipleship and self-denial with moralistic censoring of the joy and wholeness of life. No, the denial about which Jesus speaks is a way of life that believes that self-reliance and self-sufficiency and self-security cannot ever bring true joy or genuine well-being, cannot bring us to our true, best selves.

⚜⚜⚜⚜⚜⚜⚜⚜⚜

We are endlessly urged by our culture to imagine that we *can* make ourselves whole with all our amazing capacities, or that we must make ourselves whole so that we may stay in control of our lives and our destinies. And I suspect that this temptation of self-trust is more powerful in the West because of our technological capacity (much of which we turn to armaments) in seeking to secure ourselves, and more powerful among the affluent because we have more access and imagine we can purchase and use and control as much of the world as we can get our hands on. In our technological self-deception, moreover, we isolate ourselves, disregard our neighbor, forget how to care, how to be generous, how to be compassionate, and our humanness ends in a destruction that is deathly. The loss of self-risking neighborliness produces many pathologies, among them the surge of violence that always comes with a loss of neighborliness.

⚜⚜⚜⚜⚜⚜⚜⚜⚜

To deny is to break with those temptations that are so conventional among us. It means to break intellectually with too much certitude, as though we already know all the solutions; to break culturally, which requires giving up our sense of superiority; to break politically with our notions of security and advantage; to break economically with our capacity for a no-surprise, no-intrusion environment. To deny is to see and accept that at our core, we are born for mystery that includes both gift and cost, threat and surprise. God does God's transformative, Easter work precisely among those who yield their self-control to the slippage of God's mysterious gift of life. The notion of self-control must be denied in order to receive life as a gift, for life as a gift is the only life that can be full and joyous and satisfying.

⚜⚜⚜⚜⚜⚜⚜⚜⚜

We in the West have almost gained it all, all the money, all the know-how, all the markets, all the techniques. And we are nearly soulless. What we have gained in our cross-less glory is nothing compared to what we have lost.

⚜⚜⚜⚜⚜⚜⚜⚜⚜

The Bible is not morbid, but it does believe that we must think seriously about our death in order to live our life well. . . . In biblical terms, death is no flat, one-dimensional matter, and therefore life is also a rich and complex possibility. Both death and life come to mean something in biblical faith that the world does not easily understand.

⚜⚜⚜⚜⚜⚜⚜⚜⚜

Believers are always required to make two moves. The first move is to admit honestly the depth of the crisis: No denial, no pretense, no cover-up. . . . The second move is to wait, to trust, to submit, to cry out in pain and make petition. The second move is to open the place of loss to the power of God. And where we are able to practice such honest openness, God comes. God can move against our trouble, our loss, our defeat. Death, as the Bible treats it, is to arrive at the end of all our resources, and ceasing to care. Now life comes after our resources fail. There are resources available other than ours, that move us beyond ourselves into the energy, freedom, and joy of God. It is good news that comes only in the midst of our deep honesty about defeat.

❧❧❧❧❧❧❧

What shall we turn loose of? Well, I imagine in a variety of ways, our turning loose concerns our long-held privilege and our acceptance of privileged entitlement. That privilege is quite male, quite white, quite Western, quite controlling of the colonies to our advantage. But imagine with evangelical eyes to see that the world of privilege, on which we have counted for so long, is now emptied of its old possibilities. We can sense the loss of the old world, and we dare imagine it is God's subtraction.

❧❧❧❧❧❧❧

Patience is not resignation. It is not saying with cynicism, "Well, you just have to put up with things." No, patience is the capacity to stay at the vision, to work at it all the time, every day, even when the odds are long. Those who most closely follow Jesus know that they work uphill against long odds, against injustice, uncaring, and violence, but do not quit. Such patience, grounded in God's goodness, has to include some dimension of impatience, to be ready now and then to say, "Enough already, this has to change." The mix of patience and impatience knows that we are at it for the long haul, waiting for the full coming of God's rule, but waiting with active expectation.

❧❧❧❧❧❧❧

We know the cruciality of grief, but we must find ways to let the grief touch all the hurt. It is a deep ideological pathology among us that we contain the grief in private realities of guilt and individual measures of hurt. But the grief binds us all—oppressed and oppressor, victim and perpetrator—and we are driven to common tears that break beyond our private tears to cry for the whole world.

⚜⚜⚜⚜⚜⚜⚜⚜

We must face the evangelical outcome of tears genuinely shed. Our grief work does not lead simply to a new square one unencumbered, as if now we will start again. Rather it leads us to a new move from the other side, of a God who intends something of life and who acts, who takes initiative and with a kind of rhetorical finality can say, I have planned it, it will be. I have purposed it, it will stand. I have announced it, who will resist it? And there is a deep silence in response, for the defeated powers grow silent. God will out. And we are privileged to act in the new space of this sovereign decree, wholly new people on our way rejoicing.

Chapter Twelve

Faithful Practices

We are the ones who gather regularly to give thanks. We call it Eucharist, in which we gather at the table of thanks, and we eat and drink in gratitude for all the surges of new life that God enacts in this Eastered world.

❧❧❧❧❧❧❧❧

Bread is the central agenda of our faith and, therefore, of our work:

Bread has to do with the entire ecosystem of creation, from the management of water and soil to the breeding of good seed.

Bread has to do with the most elemental staple of all human diet, in every culture, for every economic class, the concrete guarantee that human life can be sustained, regardless of status or resources, aware that if not shared, human life is placed in jeopardy.

Bread, the kind we watch being blessed and broken when we are gathered at communion table, is a sign that the most elemental stuff of the earth is infused with Holy Mystery, so our work is to see how the life-giving generosity of heaven is at work in the life-needing appetites of the earth, an issue peculiar for theological types like us.

Bread, in the rougher language of the street, of course means "money," and by its reference we are introduced into the entire world of the economy, of credit and debt, of mortgages and interest rates, of spending and budgets and tax incentives and market management and the high cost of neighborliness.

⚜⚜⚜⚜⚜⚜

Baptism is a first-level act in the church, perhaps the first-level act that precedes and defines all else in the church: It is an act of water and word that signifies God's coming to us in our need, and making us true selves treasured as the apple of God's eye. It is an act whereby we are situated in the gospel, given an identity and a worth that the world can neither give nor take away from us. It is a sign of a promise from God, that God will be for us and give us a good future, even in spite of ourselves. It is an act of solidarity, whereby we are brought deeply into the body of the church with many brothers and sisters, some like us, some quite unlike us. It is an act whereby we have been marked as a member of that body, a beloved, treasured child of God.

⚜⚜⚜⚜⚜⚜

The visible practice of Sabbath rest that disengages from the pursuit of commodity is an insistent assertion about the nature of being human. The pause for receptivity of holy gifts that are inscrutably given is a break in the rigor of production and consumption. Taking time to be human is a deep contrast to the drivenness of the acquisitive life that is always on the make and that ends in fatigue that has no energy for humane living.

The practice of prayer that binds us in love to God and in love to neighbor beyond our small claim is the resolve to live life on terms other than our own. Such yielding to the largeness of God's rule is a challenge to much of our tribalism, for our conventional tribalism limits the scope of concern and teaches us that to yield is to lose.

❖❖❖❖❖❖❖

In Christian practice we have a way to mark that miracle of being named and guaranteed from all eternity by God's own love. We call it baptism. It is not magic; but it is a sacrament. That is, it is a deep poetic gesture that expresses what we can hardly say or believe. Adult or infant, we do with water and word; we celebrate a naming as a "child of promise" that defeats all fear. The ones under the waters of baptism come up unafraid, because the threat of being forgotten, abandoned, lost, displaced, is overcome by the waters.

❖❖❖❖❖❖❖

Praise is a statement that life is open, that humaneness is possible, that there are resources beyond self and newness still to be given that we do not imagine. Something is happening in our culture that precludes serious singing. We may settle for television jingles and other empty clichés, but real singing seems to have a blanket over it that reduces voice to a mumble, or we imagine that we should hire people with better voices to do our singing for us, but praise is never a spectator sport. The great enemy of praise in our time is despair, the sense that newness is not possible, that what has been will be, that there is no new thing under the sun, that what will be given has been given, that life consists in grimly moving the pieces around, that life is essentially a hopeless holding action in which possibility is closed and imagination is stifled.

Praise is a question to the church. Do you think life is open to miracle and gift that is not generated by us? Indeed, the church might do well to organize its life to see whether we can, for the sake of the gospel, be organized against despair into a singing community of hope.

❧❧❧❧❧❧❧❧❧

We have emptied our common life of serious liturgy. But until we recover the power of our particular community metaphors, we are left only with the liturgies of press conferences, professional football, and the 700 Club. Jeremiah and Second Isaiah are struggling to reclaim Israel's imagination. It is only our shared imagination that lets us move into God's hurt and God's hope and then to be changed. And when we abandon our characteristic shared imagination in the church, we succumb to the flat healings and the hopeless grieving of the world. But we have been entrusted with more, with that which moves beyond private, controlled agenda to the great cosmic ache and the great lordly gift of God.

❧❧❧❧❧❧❧❧❧

The task and goal of worship, accompanied by education and pastoral care, is to move our lives from the dominant version of reality to the sub-version so that our old certitudes will have been subverted by the work of the Spirit. Judged by the dominant version, life in the sub-version is vulnerable and foolish and exposed. But the sub-version in the end cannot be judged by the dominant version. In the end, it is judged by the truth of the gospel, by the reality of God whom we attest, and by the truth of our own lives in the image of that God. We are endlessly seduced out of that truth by the dominant version, and so we return again to worship to recite and receive this sub-version that is the truth of our life and the truth of the world.

❧❧❧❧❧❧❧❧

Sabbath—actual, concrete, visible, regular discipleship—is a sign. It signifies an alternative life. It is an invitation to get our public performance in sync with our inner selves so that there need be no gnashing of teeth or self-hatred or sense of failure. But it is more than public and personal congruity; Sabbath is an invitation to get our public performance and our personal brooding both in sync together with our true self in the gospel:

> To come to trust in assured abundance that characterizes our creation;
> To embrace freedom that is given that our culture resists.

❧❧❧❧❧❧❧❧

Let the church be a community of praise. This community has One to praise. We praise the One who made us and makes us and watches over us and cares for us more than we care for ourselves. When this praise is voiced, it is not mere rhetoric or dramatic activity or self-healing through psychology. This praise matters for it acknowledges that heaven and earth are shaped and postured in a certain way. The One praised matters in fact as much as the ones who praise. The One praised is to be trusted with our common life. The One praised is to be trusted with the well-being of the community, with the security of our common life, with the safety of our society. The One praised is faithful to all generations, including this generation. That lets us leave off our despair. Praise turns us from despair to generosity and compassion, and finally to embrace justice and righteousness in the world.

⚜⚜⚜⚜⚜⚜

God decides to enter into the messy conflictedness of human history. In doing this pledge, God eschews an easy supernaturalism and takes on the hard tasks of history. God shuns any comfortable Gnosticism and engages the fleshly reality of love. God refuses Docetism and says that the life of the body politic is real life. And in that life, it is hard historical work, acts of justice, exhibits of mercy, practices of compassion, one case at a time.

⚜⚜⚜⚜⚜⚜

The gospel intends that grateful people should be differently in the world:

- The faithful Savior intends that in a society of resentment that craves vengeance, this treasured people will practice forgiveness, because we have been forgiven.
- The faithful Savior intends that in a world of parsimony and scarcity, these hair-counted people will practice endless generosity, sharing without grudge, not needing to keep for self.
- The faithful Savior intends that in our society of exclusivism that wants to fend off any not like us, that we should practice hospitality, open welcome to those different from us.
- The faithful Savior intends that in a world of exploitative greed, the protected people should care about concrete justice issues, about housing and

health and prison reform and that whole list of gospel issues that call us beyond ourselves.

❧❧❧❧❧❧❧❧

Generosity. Hospitality. Forgiveness. When we resolve to live that way, the neighborhood is transformed.

But I do not need to tell you that that is not how the world comes at us:

- The world is not generous. The world tends to be parsimonious and stingy, not sharing, but everyone out for his own gain. And Christians are called to generosity in that very world of selfishness.
- The world is not hospitable, but really wants to expel all those unlike us, so that nations keep producing refugees of those who need to be expelled, and we get very nervous about immigrants among us, especially when they claim any kind of entitlement among us. And until very recently, even Presbyterians acted as though gay people were strangers to be excluded. Those unlike us threaten us, and Christians are called, in such a world, to extend hospitality.
- The world is a place of hard-nosed vengeance in which you get what you have coming to you and nothing more, no free lunch, no open space, no slack in retaliation. And Christians, in such a world of harsh calculation, are called to break those cycles with generous acts of forgiveness.

❧❧❧❧❧❧❧❧

The world that is held in Christ's hand is a world filled with thanks, always knowing and expressing and enacting gratitude. The Father has endowed us with a share of the new world; the creator God has given us the gift of life, the gift that keeps on giving. Gratitude is an act of rendering our life back to the God of all gifts.

⚜⚜⚜⚜⚜⚜⚜

Christian worship is an act of human imagination that voices, advocates, and insists upon a gospel perception of all lived reality. The substance of worship is to tell the story in the form of many smaller stories, all of them featuring Yahweh as the key character. The purpose of such reportage on past events of miracle is precisely so that the contemporary congregation, many seasons later, may participate as directly as possible in a world of miraculous fidelity to which the text attests and which Yahweh decisively inhabits.

⚜⚜⚜⚜⚜⚜⚜

Sabbath breaks the great cycle of social contrasts and social differentiation. Sabbath rest—work stoppage—requires no expensive equipment as for polo or scuba diving or rappelling. Just stop. Just breathe. Just wait. Just rest. Just receive. Just receive life as a gift. And do so in an amazing equality, because as you look around, all manner of creatures—oxen and donkeys and livestock—and zebras and pandas and oak trees and thistle and kudzu break from the pattern of production.

⚜⚜⚜⚜⚜⚜⚜

The practice of faithful worship is more odd than we often take it to be, familiar as it is to us. In recent time much of that oddness has been relinquished in the church, in a seductive attempt to be current, popular, alternative, or entertaining. It is, I submit, a major task of the church to receive, acknowledge, and respond to the oddness of our odd holy partner.

Worship is an act of poetic imagination that aims to reconstrue the world. It is an act of imagination, by which I mean it presents lived reality in images, figures, and metaphors that defy our conventional structures of plausibility and that host alternative scenarios of reality that cut beyond our conventional perceptual field. This act of imagination that offers an alternative world is, perforce, a poetic act; that is, it is given us in playful traces and hints that come at us sideways and that do not conform to any of our usual categories of understanding or explanation. The practice of such poetic imagination that invites us playfully to alternative reality is deeply rooted in old texts, old memories, and old practices; it nonetheless requires contemporary, disciplined, informed imagination to sustain alternative vision.

⚜⚜⚜⚜⚜⚜⚜⚜

The glory of Yahweh is not simply bland and ordinary, or enthusiastic religion. Affirmation of God's glory is always a counterstatement. It is not only pro-Yahweh, but it is determinedly anti. We do not know what to sing for, if we do not understand what we sing against. The glory of God is not sung in a vacuum, but in a context where much is at risk.

⚜⚜⚜⚜⚜⚜⚜⚜

Our life is to be one like God's life: subject to weakness without denial, in solidarity with humanity in its need, generously lavish with what we have, ready to deal gently. We have to learn again that nonviolence is the way to well-being, and the violence of war, of capital punishment, of economic assaults on the poor, of road rage, are the path to death; that generosity creates neighborhoods, and greed results in hostility and alienation; that slow face-to-faceness creates well-being, and that we cannot in any case win the rat race.

❧❧❧❧❧❧❧❧❧

Evangelical obedience is not coercive. It is more like new, enraptured love, in which one seeks out the will of the loved one in eagerness to please, finding such obedience to be sheer delight and joy, even if it inconveniences, costs, disrupts, and unsettles.

❧❧❧❧❧❧❧❧❧

The holiness of the church does not consist in true doctrine that everyone accepts. It does not consist in true morality that everyone embraces. We know of course that the church has often specialized in doctrine and morality. But the truth is that the holiness of the baptized community consists in the habits of generosity, grace in speaking, and tenderhearted forgiveness. Imagine such an agenda for the church: generosity, grace, forgiveness. These are the marks of baptism, these are the marks of Jesus, these are the shapes of our new life in Christ. The truth of the church, dramatized in baptism, is that our life is so safe that we can trust ourselves in the world. And when we do that, the world will see our holiness, our righteousness, our life in God. That is who we are. That's us! And we are not like them, because our life in generosity, grace, and forgiveness is in the image of God. By our life, God is honored and the world is healed. That's us!

❧❧❧❧❧❧❧❧❧

The baptismal conversation is not dishonest about our hurt, does not deceive about our failure, does not deny about the violence all around of which we are apart. The baptismal conversation does, however, place in the midst of hurt, failure, and violence this other word which has been spoken over us, spoken before us, spoken against us, spoken on our behalf. This other word is *hesed*, God's steadfast love which overruns our hurt, outdistances our failure, supersedes our violence, outflanks our sin. In the end, because that other word is true, our words are changed. Our words are now serious speech, ready in hope and confidence for a new obedience. Baptism is a decision to stop the mindless preoccupation of the world and focus on how the world will be, when recast in fidelity.

❧❧❧❧❧❧❧❧

Pharaoh takes many forms. Imagine Pharaoh as a hovering parent long since dead but hovering. Pharaoh as colleagues more competent than us who set the bar very high and who, by their very existence, summon us to greater excellence than we have yet reached. Pharaoh as approval giver who does not give it easily—and always reluctantly and grudgingly, so that we ourselves up the quota to satisfy performance. The church as Pharaoh who will never say, "Well done, enter into my rest." Rather it keeps available an endless list of duties, and we cast as the duty officer of every day.

So imagine Sabbath. Imagine Sabbath as the breaking of the cycle of coercion. Imagine Sabbath as the great day of equality when all of God's creatures sit quietly and wait and receive gifts of healing and nourishment and well-being. It is promised to us that this God of grace constitutes a summons to a different time management at the center of which stands restfulness. The work of the creator-redeemer God gets done, even though that God of Sabbath is like you at rest, unhurried and unharried.

Imagine the church as a Sabbath-keeping community that is a drastic contrast to the world of productivity. Imagine that the peasants are waiting and watching for the seventh day, and we model it. Imagine that the big-time players who are coerced by their own success also wonder if there is an alternative, and imagine that clergy as leaders are to embody and model the reality of restfulness that is rooted in God's self-giving love, this God who is a lively, life-giving alternative to every Pharaoh.

⚜⚜⚜⚜⚜⚜⚜

The Creator promises and guarantees abundance, and Sabbath is the day we luxuriate in that abundance as a gift which we do not need to perform or possess or acquire or achieve . . . because it is a gift!

⚜⚜⚜⚜⚜⚜⚜

Sabbath practice is to break the denial and become "truth-tellers," for the truth will make us Sabbath free.

- Tell the truth, free of ideological rancor, about the pain of the world for it is the truth of pain on the cross through which the world is saved.
- Tell the truth about the pain of the ancient slaves who were reduced to silence in Egypt, and the whole history of enslavement down to the contemporary pain of economic bondage and racial shut-out and gender selfishness.
- Tell the truth about the pain of the destruction of Jerusalem through arrogant, obtuse political-military policy and the whole history of self-destruction enacted through military arrogance.
- Tell the truth of the pain of exile and displacement and grief, of the whole history of refugees and

displaced persons who ache for not belonging. And then give a hint that even we are among those displaced people in our ache.

- Tell the truth about the lament Psalms and the absence of God and the indifference of God that violates the claims of the catechism, an absence and an indifference that are known everywhere in an honest church.

- Tell the truth and you will end the power of denial, the frantic need to make it right, the anxiety about augmenting the "inadequate" abundance of the creation.

We always stand, as did Jesus, before the governor who notoriously asked, "What is truth?" The truth withheld from the wise and given to babes is that pain is the matrix of newness. Tell the truth without pious protectiveness, without ideological reductionism, stay close to the text, tell the truth and you will find the weariness easing as you come clean to the one who is the truth, and the way and the life, a way of pain, a life of vulnerability.

❧❦❧❦❧❦❧❦❧

We take prayer so easily and routinely, but we should notice what a bold, revolutionary act this prayer is. Prayer is not pious abdication. It is a daring maneuver whereby the speaker breaks the categories of trouble and shatters the closed world of threat. It is a defiant alternative to sinking into the deep waters. In a world where there is only me, prayer is a nervy act of insistence that makes no sense. The only people who can do the daring act of prayer are those who know that the world is visited, attended to, and occupied by our advocate who can overpower death.